Mills, Mollies & Marl Pits

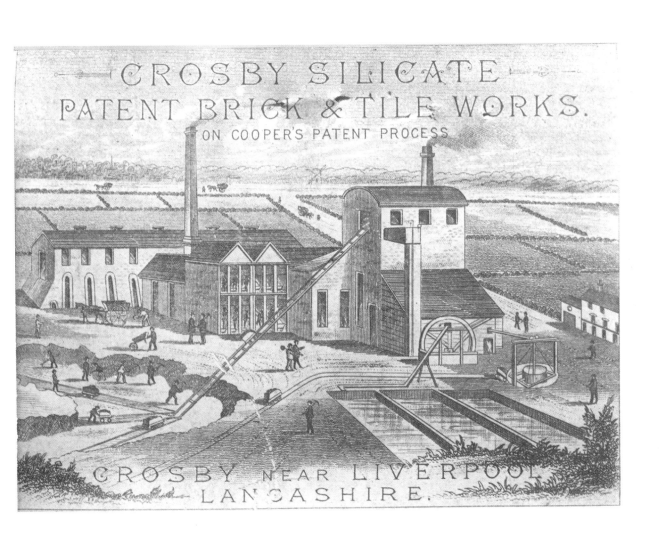

Mills, Mollies
& Marl Pits

The story of the township of Great Crosby

JOHN COCHRANE

CROSBY VILLAGE PUBLISHING

To my wife Jenny, born and bred in Crosby,
for putting up with a newcomer of only
thirty-five years

First published in Great Britain in 2005 by
Crosby Village Publishing
42 Liverpool Road
Crosby L23 SF

A CIP catalogue record for this book is available from the British
Library

ISBN-13: 9780955174308
ISBN-10: 0955174309

Printed by Poplar Services of St. Helens

Details of illustration copyright are listed on page 7. Every effort
has been made to trace all copyright holders, but if any have been
inadvertently overlooked, the author would be pleased to make the
necessary credits at the first opportunity.

CONTENTS

ACKNOWLEDGEMENTS

My biggest thank you must be to the staff of the Local History department at Crosby Library. They have provided me with all manner of scraps of information as well as use of archives produced with unfailing courtesy and assistance. Similarly the staff at the Liverpool Record Office

The people of Crosby especially clergyman, licensees, business owners, school staff, etc. who have also responded to my demands on their valuable time.

Brenda Murray, Tom Heath, Brian Vincent, who has provided the line drawings, Bob Wright, of the Little Crosby Museum, and Rod Stringer with his knowledge of all things maritime, especially concerning the 'Titanic', Steve Pritchard of Pritchard Books for his encouragement and advice and Clare Churly who designed this book.

PICTURE ACKNOWLEDGEMENTS

John Cochrane 13, 25, 28, 30, 43, 45, 52, 67, 71, 93.

Crosby Herald 64.

Tom Heath 3, 17, 54, 59, 61.

Liverpool Record Office 32

Sefton Local History Archive 1, 4, 9, 21, 27, 29, 49, 55, 58, 62, 70, 74, 76, 83, 84.

Brian Vincent 23, 31, 60, 73.

Every effort has been made to trace copyright holders, but if any have been inadvertantly overlooked, the author would be pleased to make the necessary credits at the first opportunity.

LEFT Original site of the cross in Crosby Village.

INTRODUCTION

There has not been a comprehensive history of Crosby since 1936. Not only has the area changed considerably since then but so has the increase in the thirst for knowledge of the local history of the community.

The purpose of this account is to outline the story of the area known as Great Crosby, and its rise from a small village near the Lancashire coast to what many would consider to be a virtual suburb of Liverpool.

What and where, exactly is Great Crosby? For the purposes of this account it approximates to the boundaries of the old Urban District. This also includes those geographical areas with rather vague boundaries such as Blundellsands and Brighton-le-sands. We cannot however ignore the history of the surrounding areas especially the influence of its near neighbour Little Crosby. The township of Great Crosby officially ceased to exist on the formation of the Borough of Crosby in 1937. Crosby itself had its demise in 1974 with the establishment of the Metropolitan Borough of Sefton.

In spite of these many changes Great Crosby has managed to maintain a character of its own. It has a story worth telling.

My hope is that this short history will make the reader stop, look around, and see something on even the most familiar walk.

RIGHT Crosby Windmill 1814–c1895.

CHAPTER 1
BEGINNING

The history of any locality has to begin with the first written words, but we must start with an earlier, perhaps more speculative account.

About 10,000 years ago the last of the great glaciers slowly began their grinding retreat northwards across Britain. The Mesolithic hunter-gatherers, who had been enjoying the sunnier climes of Europe, steadily followed them in pursuit of pastures new. Britain was not an island then and to walk across what was to become the Channel was comparatively easy. However, as the ice melted, the sea levels rose and, over the centuries, the Atlantic linked up with the North Sea. Britain then became the island fortress that has affected so much of her later history. These huge volumes of melted water brought down from the north the silt, which formed the clay and sandstone so typical of the Lancashire area. As the ice melted the tundra of Southern England moved steadily and remorselessly north, the wind blown mosses retreated before the birch and heather, and later by the forests of oak, elm, and hazel. The deer and wild boar followed the giant sloth and the woolly mammoth, and the first Britons found better hunting, food, and climate.

The area we now know as South West Lancashire was an inhospitable place – a land of salt marshes, sand dunes and peat bog – a land of mists and penetrating rain, but over the millennia man slowly tamed it. As the climate ebbed and flowed, although always getting steadily warmer, these early men hunted and fished along the shores of the Irish Sea. Over the last fifty years or so there have been many discoveries of their presence, none more fascinating than their actual footprints. The giant aurochs, the wolves, the deer and the wild boar all left their marks in the soft silt. These were baked by the hot sun, and then preserved by the covering of wind blown sand. Amongst these animal prints were the human ones, sometimes overlaying them. Careful measurement gave heights of between 1.4 and 1.6 metres for these Stone Age people and they have been dated to about 4–5,000 years old.

Three thousand years ago the Celtic people stirred from their birthplaces in Central Europe and brought the Iron and Bronze Ages into Britain. In 1996 a Bronze Age wooden roadway was discovered on the beach towards Hightown. This was a comparatively sophisticated structure and may have been built across the marshes to reach fish traps, or possibly even boats. As the Roman Empire expanded, the Celts were pushed out into the fringes of Europe. The Romans found little to their taste, in Britain, especially the climate. They certainly kept away from the marshy, wet Lancashire coast. The Roman road ran northwards from Chester keeping to the high ground of central Lancashire crossing the

Mersey at Warrington and thence via Wigan and Walton-le-dale to Lancaster. In 1866 a number of Roman coins were found in Formby dated to around 330 A.D. It is possible that these were left by a group exploring the area or maybe using the route that went from Deva (Chester) through the Wirral and across the marshes that are now the Mersey estuary. Many of the Celtic people settled in Ireland, and, as the Roman Empire expanded, they made many trade contacts. By about 400 AD the traders were followed by the first Christian missionaries. As often happened, the local pagan rituals were grafted on; the Celts acceptance of Christianity evinced by their reverence for the symbol of the cross. As the Empire collapsed a scattered few made their way across the Irish Sea and settled in South West Lancashire, still a poor cheerless place. These were probably from a tribal group called the Setantii, 'dwellers in watery lands'. They hunted, fished, and cleared some of the scrub forest to plant cereals. They may have found that living in such a backwater gave them peace and security. These people built huts of inter-twined branches and twigs smeared with clay to fill in the gaps – so-called wattle and daub. They used fire for heating and cooking, metal tipped spears for hunting, and reared horses as beasts of burden, dogs for hunting, and sheep for the wool. This wool was made into clothes on very primitive looms, although the main reliance for garments was still animal skins. The cereals that they grew were crushed with

stones and baked into bread and cakes. Very little of this remains except some of their place names – Alt for a stream and Ince for a water meadow, and their profusion of large crosses placed at every meeting place and crossroads, and for guidance to travellers

With the gradual withdrawal of the Roman influence during the first five hundred years of the Christian era, the island of Britain became a target for the marauding tribes from Scandinavia. The Angles came from Denmark, reaching the west coast of Lancashire by about 650 A.D. but to a large extent left the poor coastlands to the Celts, and settled on the higher ground to the east. For the next three hundred years the area to the north of the Mersey was nominally part of the Christian kingdom of Northumbria, which was in almost permanent conflict with pagan Mercia to the south.

Meanwhile, over in Norway there was disruption and in-fighting amongst those great warriors and explorers, the Vikings. The Vikings that ended up in South West Lancashire were not marauding raiders but, by the standards of the time, peaceful refugees. The internecine conditions in 8th century Norway caused the Viking population to spread westwards across the seas to Scotland, Ireland, Iceland, and even North America. Many settled in the Dublin area but were in permanent conflict with the Celtic population. Tired of war and battles most of the Viking families set sail across the Irish Sea. Place names, and even many current surnames, reflect settlements from the River Dee up to the Scottish border. These settled on the poorer marsh areas rather than on the hillier and more productive areas to the east. These they left to the Angles and Saxons – this is hardly the attitude of the violent conqueror!

The idea of Vikings being 'pagan' and 'heathen' bent on the destruction of any evidence of Christianity, whether buildings or persons, needs clarifying. Celtic Ireland had become steadily more Christian since the fourth century. The Vikings had done much destruction when they first arrived, but settling down and intermarrying produced a mixture of the two religious traditions. Christianity eventually became the dominant partner. By the time of the landings in Lancashire in the early 900s, the Vikings showed great respect for the Cross, and other Celtic artefacts. Evidence of their conversion can be seen in place names such as Formby, Kirkby, Ormskirk, and of course Crosby, as well as the Harkirk in Little Crosby.

By the late 900s the Vikings had considerable control over most of England. In 1002 Wulfric called the area *Landa betwae Ribbel and Moerse*. They organized their domains into areas called counties, of varying sizes, and thence into hundreds. A hundred was an approximate amount of land that could sustain one hundred families. The hundred of West Derby covered a great swathe of South West Lancashire, which gives some idea of how sparse was the population at that time.

The next great invasion was that of the Normans. They were of Viking stock and their leader, William the Conqueror, had, at least in his eyes, a legitimate claim to the throne of England. He realised however that his small Norman army could not conquer, and hold, all of that country. He had no option but to recruit a ragbag of mercenaries from all over Europe and all he could offer them was land. William quickly subdued England and gave most of Lancashire to Roger of Poitou, including the hundred of West Derby. Roger saw little point in getting involved with the petty local affairs so he allowed the original owner, Uctred, an Angle, to run the area as he saw fit, as long as he provided the regular tax of corn, pigs, eggs, or whatever else Roger required. The King saw his greatest problem as the Celts of Wales and Scotland. About 1080, for strategic reasons, he took back much of the Welsh border regions, including most of Lancashire and Cheshire as his own domains. The Domesday survey of 1085 does not mention the King's lands in any detail. There is a brief description of Uctred's holdings, under the overall control of Roger of Poitou, which included the manors of Roby, Knowsley, Kirkby, Crosby, Aughton and Maghull. Crosby is spelt 'Crosebi'. (The spelling is recorded as Crosseby in 1176, Major Crossby in 1211, and Mickle Crosseby in 1292). Roger soon regained his lands, and when William Rufus followed his father on to the English throne in 1087, he increased that knight's holdings until he owned virtually all of Lancashire. In 1102 Roger finally forfeited all his lands to the current king, Henry I. The most powerful influence in the area was, without doubt, the family of Molyneux, the lords of the manor of Sefton. William de Molines (from Moulins, in France) came over with the Conqueror and was granted the manor of Toxteth. His influence increased with the gifts of other parts of Lancashire as well as in the rest of the country. His son Robert gained a large part of Litherland by 1120. Richard Molyneux was knighted by Henry III in 1256, and by then owned much of Sefton, Thornton, Litherland and Little Crosby. By this time the parish of Sefton, based on St. Helen's church extended to all of Great and Little Crosby. The first mention of Great Crosby, as Magna Crossebie is in the Pipe Rolls of 1172. The virtually uninhabited area known today as Great Crosby, passed from king to earl to knight and back to king until about 1192, when it became the property of the Earl of Mortain, better known as Prince John, who held the manor of Great Crosby for King Richard I, while he was away on a cru-sade. John leased the manor to a forester, Robert of Ainsdale in 1212 for 100 shillings (£5) per year. The annual Pipe Rolls since then listed Crosby (actually Little Crosby) separate from Great Crosby. The leasehold of Great Crosby stayed in Robert's family for several generations. His great grandson, also called Robert, took over the lease in 1277. He was noted for his distinctive blond hair and was called Robert Blondell, later corrupted to Blundell. The family, now called the Blundells, acquired much influence but were

ABOVE Boundary stone junction of Oaklands and Little Crosby Road.

still subservient to the Molyneux family. Then, in 1362, Agnes Molyneux married David Blundell, and the two most important families in the Crosby area were united.

During the fifteenth century there was often conflict between the two families, especially over the rights of strays and wreckage. These conflicts often ended in violence and even attempted murder. At this time Great Crosby consisted of a few scattered farms, which paid rent to the steward of the manor, and a group of cottages in the area now Crosby Village. The men in of the cottages worked on the farms, the women made bread and brewed beer. This tiny hamlet was often known as

Crosby Hillock. Religious life was centred on the church of St. Helen, at Sefton. In about 1460 there was a dispute between Henry Blundell and the tenant farmers of Great Crosby. An adjudicator was chosen who was acceptable to both Blundell, as leaseholder, and Sir Richard Molyneux, who still acted as steward of the land for the King. The adjudicator took sixteen of the tenants and rode round the village setting up boundary stones. These were triangular in shape. One still exists on Little Crosby Road near the junction with Oaklands Avenue. The names Little Crosby and Great Crosby were originally carved on the stone but were defaced in 1940 to confuse possible German paratroops. Henry Blundell followed the line of the stones and dug a ditch to mark the first boundary of Great Crosby. This ditch was known as Thornback Pool. Keeping these ditches clear was very important if flooding of arable land was to be contained. Nicholas Blundell's diary recounts checking on the men sent to clear this pool and found it blocked and the men drinking in the alehouse. A bridge was built to carry Little Crosby Lane (now Road), over the Thornback Pool. Its collapse, in 1665, caused flooding of the Blundell land at Oaklands. In an out of court settlement the people of Great Crosby would, in future, be responsible for the repair of the bridge, and William Blundell would not charge for the flood damage. A bridge made from large flat stones from the Delph quarry in Little Crosby to be called the Wheat Hey

Stone Platt, lasted for many years with no trouble. William Blundell, who owned the quarry, charged the farmers of Great Crosby eight shillings for the stone. Between 1461 and the establishment of the Great Crosby Health Board, in 1862, local government was centred on the Halmcote Court at the village cross. By 1538 the inhabitants were in a position to hold annual elections for officers. Most important was the reeve. He was a type of chief magistrate, and his equivalent over a county was called a shire-reeve, from which we get the word sheriff. There were also two constables, four sworn men to act as jurors, two supervisors of wrecks, and two ale-tasters. The supervisors of wrecks were very important in an area where the combination of prevailing north west winds, silted up channels, and outcrops of rock, took their toll of passing ships. Arguments over who was entitled to what cargoes or parts of ships were a feature of the age. The ale-tasters were sixteenth century versions of trading standards officers. It was women's work to make beer, the so-called ale-wives, or brew-sters (the feminine form of brewer). They often cheated on measure, or were guilty of watering down the beer. In many mystery plays the ale-wife was thrown into the fires of Hell for watering or giving short measure.

From 1580 the Molyneux family were entitled to keep all income from rents and fines in the lands under their stewardship for an annual payment of £13 13s 8?d, payable to the crown. Royal ownership of Great Crosby came to an end in 1625 when Charles I sold it to the Molyneux family for £12,000.

The many Enclosure Acts largely upheld the rights of Great Crosby's tenant farmers. In principle these divided the large areas of common land into individual small-holdings, later to become family farms, and were made legal by individual Acts of Parliament. At this time Great Crosby was divided between the farmlands to the east, and the poor salt marshes towards the sea. The dividing line was roughly Liverpool Road and College Road (then called Marsh Lane). In 1602 the government of Queen Elizabeth I gave local rights to about 200 acres of marshlands to be drained and enclosed. This was land between Seaforth and Blundellsands. In 1654 William Blundell marked out an area on the Crosby Marsh for a racecourse. This was based on an older site used for horse racing since 1577. The marshy area had no value as it was and few farmers could contemplate the expense of drainage. It is not surprising that no serious effort to recover this area was made until 1816. In that year the land was awarded at a meeting in the Ship Inn in Warrenhouse Road. The Ship Inn also saw the setting up of a more organized form of local government. At a meeting in the inn about 1750,(although called the Ship Inn this may have referred to the Ship Victory Inn in Waterloo), all the smallholders of the township had to attend or face a fine. The following officials were elected. To attend to small offences, the straying of animals and allowing one's holding to fall

into disrepair, twelve jurymen were sworn in. There was also a village constable, a chapel reeve, a keeper of the village pound, an ale-taster, and an astronomer. This last official's duties appeared to be some sort of weather forecaster and making sure that certain days in the religious and agricultural calendar were adhered to. It is doubtful whether any of the cottages had a calendar on the wall! More serious cases were referred to the Court Baron of the West Derby Hundred based at Farnworth.

The Molyneux family held the land until 1798 when it was sold to the Blundells.

The city of Liverpool in the seventeenth century was a very minor port whose main activity was the passenger trade with Ireland. It could not compete with Chester's trade with Ireland, or with the lucrative North American routes operated from Bristol. As the eighteenth century dawned the River Dee was silting up making the viability of Chester as a port in doubt. Coupled with the meteoric rise in the industrial base of south Lancashire, and its export potential, the demise of Chester and Bristol was only a matter of time. The subsequent rise of Liverpool's fortunes was reflected in the new class of *nouveau riche* merchants. The year 1709 saw the rapid development of state of the art dock facilities, and also the beginning of the slave trade. The deplorable trade in slaves, as well as what amounted to state controlled piracy against the French and Spanish, over the ensuing decades, produced even more wealthy families. And where would they build their fine houses? Many moved out into the sub-urbs, some over the Mersey to leafy Cheshire, but many looked north to the areas developing around the bracing sea air towards Southport. The only direct route to Crosby was by the Leeds and Liverpool canal, and then by carriage up Endbutt Lane, or the hazardous coach trip along the sands. The coming of the railway, in 1848, saw a rapid expansion in the number of fine houses being built in Crosby. William Blundell gave the land for the railway free of charge, to keep the smelly, smoky locomotives away from Little Crosby. He was also shrewd enough to realise that the area called Blundellsands, through which the railway now progressed, could be enclosed and drained – not for farming but for the building of residences for the new gentry. The opening of the road and public transport links, after 1900, fuelled the development even more. The population of Great Crosby doubled between 1863 and 1902, and doubled again within twenty years.

The rising population of camp followers caused the spread of houses along the Liverpool to Southport road, and into Blundellsands to the rich merchants; the carriage dealers, insurance brokers, estate agents. As well as, of course, the builders, joiners and plumbers who required the smaller houses in between. These spread from Liverpool Road to College Road, and north-wards from Coronation Road.

The area to the south of Great Crosby was a very popular place for sea bathing. It was called Crosby Seabank until 1815. Apparently as the Royal Hotel was under construction, the victory at Waterloo was announced. The hotel, and eventually the whole area, became known as Waterloo. Local Boards of Health were established in Waterloo-with-Seaforth in 1856, Great Crosby in 1863, and Little Crosby, in 1870. These became Urban District councils in 1894. Great Crosby adopted the 1858 Local Government Act on 24th April 1863. The nine member board of health first met in a room in the George Hotel, then in the house at No. 60 Victoria Road. Shortly after becoming an Urban District the council moved to its permanent headquarters in the Assembly Rooms, later called Alexandra Hall. By 1932 Great Crosby combined with Little Crosby and, five years later, joined with Waterloo and Seaforth to form the Borough of Crosby. This was the first borough to be given royal assent by King George VI within days of his coronation, in 1937. The main coronation festival was held in Moorside Park. The coronation service, broadcast by the BBC, was relayed over loudspeakers and was followed by a recital of gramophone music. Events included a Grand Equestrian Exhibition which included 'mounted wrestling', displays of physical training and a Monster Tug of War between A and B teams from the local health department. Two world wars had their effect on Great Crosby. The memorial to those who lost their lives in these wars was erected in Alexandra Park. In World War II the obvious main target for the

RIGHT *The Cross seen
from the village. The
white buildings are
Sawyers Cottages.*

Luftwaffe was the dockland area – Britain's link to the aid coming in from the United States. Other targets were the Birkenhead and Wallasey docks as well as gas works and several factories making parts for aircraft and munitions anywhere between Southport and Chester. Crosby had no obvious targets – Fort Crosby was never hit, and Woodvale airfield was virtually untouched. Casual attacks on suburbs were a feature of this campaign. These were either unintentional or the result of jettisoning a dangerous bomb load. It is difficult to see Rothesay Drive, Bonnington Avenue, and Tudor Road, Dorbett Drive, or the Presbyterian or Methodist churches as strategic targets. A number of government changes affected life in Crosby in the early 1970s. Comprehensive education saw the amalgamation of several schools into just three secondary schools, Manor High, Chesterfield High and Sacred Heart.

Following the Maude report on local government reorganization in the 1970s, the Metropolitan Borough of Sefton was formed within the new county of Merseyside. From April 1st 1974 the new borough extended from Bootle in the south to Southport in the north. This effectively ended Crosby's long existence as an officially recognised township.

CHAPTER 2
FARMING

From the end of the Roman Empire for three or four hundred years the Great Crosby area was in the possession of the Angles of Northumbria. The men of the villages (Sefton and Thornton date from this period) had a strip of land to grow cereals and a share of rough pasturing for hay and cattle rearing. Each hamlet was self-sufficient in food and could be turned into a temporary fortified camp, although it was more usual for the peasantry to escape into the surrounding dense forest until the marauders had gone. For many generations the local farmers accepted that whether their occupiers were Angle, Viking or Norman the seasons didn't change. The agricultural year began at Michaelmas in late September after the harvest. There were usually two fields. One for ploughing to plant winter wheat and rye, the other left with the grain stubble. Winter saw the cutting of logs for fires and the slaughter of most of the cattle and the meat salted. Candlemas, in early February saw the ploughing of the second field for beans, oats and barley to be sown at Easter. May saw the shearing of sheep, the repair of buildings, and the clearing and draining of ditches.

The Vikings continued the agricultural calendar but introduced bee-keeping and brewing as well as the making of basic furniture. They still however relied on the animals of the forest for clothes and meat. The rigid structure of lord, then thane, villain, cottar and serf, with their attendant amount of land was preserved for longer than many other parts of the country, but by the early 1400s this feudal system was disappearing fast. The farmers began to pay the lord of the manor a rent for their land and cottage and tools, knowing that should they leave the land ALL their assets returned to the lord. Very few did. An important part of medieval farming was commoner's rights. The common land was owned by the lord of the manor but small holders were allowed use of the land under certain conditions. The level of use was linked to property and individuals and was not hereditary. Estovers was the right to remove fallen timber for the repair of hedges and cottages. Dead branches could be removed from trees provided that they could be reached by a hook or a crook (the origin of the saying). Commoners were allowed to cut turf and peat for fuel and harvest dry bracken for cattle bedding. This was excellent for the job and plentiful on the moor land area of Moor Lane and Brownmoor Lane. It had one big disadvantage – it was poisonous to cattle. The moral presumably was to never send a cow to bed hungry. All wild life, which certainly included Crosby's rabbits and eels, could be taken for food. The only exception was the king's deer, not a problem in this area. Grazing rights for cattle, sheep and goats were allowed according to the number of gates between the small holding and the common land. The number of cow-gates was often an indication of the wealth of an individual farmer. In the autumn pigs were allowed to forage for beech nuts and acorns to fatten them up for winter food.

There was an increasing amount of cooperation and bartering of produce and skills, but very little actual money changed hands. All were responsible for keeping their cottages and farm implements in good repair. This bred an increasing number of specialists like thatchers and smiths who would do this maintenance in exchange for food and clothing. The building next to Hearts health club, presently Crosby Auto-electrics, was once the village smithy, the present building stood on the site of the original workshop. Another example of co-operation was the establishing of the Bullcroft on the site of what is now Alexandra Park. This was the home of one of the most important members of the community – the town bull. Whilst most of the cows were slaughtered for winter food some had to be preserved to continue the population. A healthy bull was an absolute necessity.

A vital group of specialists were the marlers. The retreating glaciers had left thousands of pockets of rich, limey clay all over the flat wetlands of Lancashire and Cheshire. Fertilisation had been practiced for centuries.

The most popular forms were animal manure, seaweed, and the ashes from burnt stubble. Marl clay however was the most prized, but the hardest to gather. The marlers travelled from district to district digging out the marl from the pits and spreading it on the fields at a rate agreed by the land owner. Because the marling of any particular field was only required every twenty years, a great occasion was made of the marlers' visit. The digging out of the marl was watched with great interest and when the clay was extracted and spread on the field the pit was decorated with garlands of flowers. Processions and dancing followed. Part of the festivities was to encourage the marlers to shout from the bottom of the pit, for which they were paid in coins or ale. Apart from the possibility of a strange echo effect it is hard to see the entertainment value in this. The description of a 1712 marl pit flowering is graphically told in Nicholas Blundell's diary. The empty pit was used for the rather barbaric sport of bull-baiting before eventually being filled with water and used for the breeding and farming of fish, especially carp. There were so many of these pits, large and small, that virtually every smallholding had one. There were several in Great Crosby into the 1960s, and one large one still exists on the corner of Cambridge Road and Victoria Road. The farm was called Big Pit Farm and generations of children have been brought to the water filled pit to feed the ducks. The farm has been replaced with the flats called Mere Park, but the original iron railings are still there. A rare road sign on the approaches to the pit are warnings for motorists to take care as the ducks frequently cross the road.

The idea of purely subsistence farming, that is a cow for milk and the capacity to grow enough to feed the cow and the family, was beginning to diversify. Sheep became popular as they were economical to keep and provided food and clothing. The wool of English sheep was much valued in the clothing factories of Europe. By the early 1500s nearly every cottage had a spinning wheel. The wool was prepared for the itinerant dealers from the local fairs who were feeding the beginnings of the woollen cloth trade of Lancashire and Yorkshire. Some individual farmers in Crosby saw the potential and became comparatively wealthy. Most of the middle class families that began to evolve from the farming stock owed their wealth to wool. Among these was the Harrison family, later to endow the first grammar school in Great Crosby.

From 1638 three individuals could be included in the original lease of the farm. When one died a small fine could be paid to the lease holder to transfer the portion to another. If no fine was paid, and the three original lessees died, the land reverted to the owner. An astute family could keep the land forever by paying these fines, a sort of early life insurance. They could even increase their land holdings by buying reverted land very cheaply.

By the 1700s much of the dense woodland and its animals had gone. In fact Crosby was virtually treeless by the time of the publication of the navigation guide to Liverpool harbour of 1771. Looking from the Wallasey side the three landmarks listed were the tower of St. Michael's church, the windmill at Little Crosby and Merchant Taylor's school, (the old building, now the girls' school). Obviously these were clearly visible from the river. Poultry farming became important. This saw the rise of fox-hunting. Also war was declared on kites and other birds of prey, although this was unjustified. They were in fact attacking snakes, rarely young chickens. Other local fauna was being considered. The drainage ditches, especially in the northern parts of Great Crosby were full of eels. These were being conserved and farmed into sniggeries (from the old dialect word snig, for an eel). Another free source of food and clothing was the largely untouched area now known as Blundellsands, which was a huge rabbit farm – the reason why the word 'warren' is often seen in the area. Weld Road, off Agnes Road was called Rabbit Road until the 1920s. Mid-winter was the ideal time for rabbit hunting when their fur was thick and they were fat for the cold weather.

Farmers had always been aware of the ups and downs of their income, not to mention the financial effects of disease amongst their flocks. Some form of insurance had existed since the early 1800s but this was formalised in the establishment of the Great Crosby Cow Club. This was founded by a Mr Ralph Bond's on 26th October 1835.

Mr. Bond's, the name is always spelt with an apostrophe. His family may be connected with the naming of Bond's Lane, later St. Lukes Road. Members were charged one shilling entry and one shilling per animal per quarter, as well as four pence for the book of rules. As a general rule the payment for the death of a cow aged one to two years was three pounds, a two to three year old, five pounds, and one older than three years, eight pounds. The rules were a complicated series of checks and balances because of the many opportunities for fraud. The local cow-doctor along with responsible members of the Club had to decide whether or not the death was genuine and not due to neglect or euthanasia. The annual meeting of the Club was held on the third Monday in January. This was followed by a dinner at a local hostelry. Attendance was compulsory and non-attendance, for any cause, meant a fine of six pence.

Shrimping was a flourishing business in the1930s and is still carried on today albeit in a much smaller way. In 1937 a shop was opened on the corner of Sussex Street and Warrenhouse Road that sold nothing but shrimps.

Much feared were the 'Cockle Mollies' who gathered cockles and cut up driftwood to sell as firewood. Rumour had it that they often chopped up the driftwood with their bare hands! They lived rough and each individual was reputedly a match for any three police constables when fighting drunk. They slept in the porches and summerhouses of the big houses in Blundellsands where they were left undisturbed. Well, would you wake one?

LEFT Moorside Farm.

CHAPTER 3
PRAYING

We have seen evidence of religious belief in the Crosby area with the arrival of the Celts, and later the Vikings, with their crosses. The site of the Harkirk chapel in the grounds of Crosby Hall is reputed to be that of an original Angle church.

For hundreds of years all religious life in Crosby and indeed for a large part of South West Lancashire was centred on the parish church of St. Helen, in Sefton. A church existed on this site since before 1170, the first date of which we have a record. It was built as a private chapel and place of burial for the Molyneux family. It became a parish church, the spire was added about 1320, and the church completely rebuilt about 1520.

The upheavals of the Reformation hardly touched this country until Henry VIII declared himself head of the Church of England in 1534. Hostility resulting in persecution vacillated between the Catholic Church and the Protestants. In 1581 Father Lawrence Johnson was hanged at for treason at Tyburn. His crime was accompanying a local youth to a Catholic College in France, although he was arrested for plotting against the queen. Father Johnson was born and brought up at Moorside Farm. The site is now occupied by No. 37 Moorside Road. The farm was demolished in the 1650s and was replaced by Moorside House, one of the largest houses in Crosby, in 1652. This building was only demolished in

1933. A small cairn and the date stone in Moorside Park marks the spot. Henry's successor Edward VI was a weak Protestant, Mary Tudor a staunch Catholic, and Elizabeth I a strong Protestant, as much for political reasons as spiritual ones. There was much persecution of Crosby's two prominent Catholic families, the Molyneuxs and the Blundells. This turmoil culminated in the excommunication of Elizabeth I by Pope Pius V in 1570. A royal edict was then issued which forbade Catholics to attend any parish church. It was also forbidden to bury Catholics on consecrated ground. About 1600 the Blundell family cleared land around the Harkirk burial ground at Crosby Hall for local Catholics. During this work, in 1611, a large Viking coin hoard was discovered. In 1890 a small chapel was built over the burial site.

In 1624 the local sheriff, complete with posse, arrived at Little Crosby to 'investigate' the activities at the Harkirk. A large fine and the confiscation of the manor's cattle was the intended punishment. The story goes that they were spotted by a miller from the top of the Little Crosby mill. The warning went out and 40 or 50 local yeoman, armed with farm implements, gave the sheriff and his men a good hiding. Those of the posse who were badly injured were looked after in a cottage that stood on the present site of St. Luke's church. This is the closest to a riot in

Crosby's history. With the exception of the Pendle Hill area Lancashire was reasonably free of the witchcraft trials that spread throughout England between 1580 and 1620. There is however a recorded trial of one Amy Roberts of Much Crosby for this crime.

Great Crosby had a scattered, but reasonably large population, many of who found the walking distance to Sefton somewhat irksome. The church was also getting over-crowded. Sometime in the early 1400s, or even earlier, a chapel of ease was established in Crosby Village. There is a mention in the Town Rolls of debts owed by St. Michael's chapel dated 1453. Although the first officially recorded date was 1564, in 1532 a certain Nicholas Johnson, with the support of Squire Blundell, built a house in the area and forbade the residents the use of the chapel for the feast of St. Michael. This feast was well meaning and of a spiritual nature, even if it did include the pagan ceremony of well-dressing. It began to transmogrify however into the notorious Goose Feast.

This chapel was an overflow of Sefton church for local people, and saved the long arduous walk on a Sunday. This became very popular for the elderly, and for everyone in the depths of winter. Baptisms continue to be held at Sefton church. The first recorded at St. Michael's was in 1749. Nothing is known of the chapel's construction except that the base of the original cross of St. Michael was retained as a baptismal font, using the waters

CROSBY CHAPEL

ABOVE Line drawing of St. Michael's chapel, Crosby Village, 1770–1835, from a painting by W. Herdman.

of the well. The site chosen was close to an ancient cross, which marked the well of St. Michael. The well was a place of pilgrimage, as it was believed that the presence of the saint endowed the waters with healing powers. As the village centre it was the place where the manorial court proclamations were made during the reign of Henry VIII. The chapel was dedicated to St. Michael of Monte Tumba. This was the Archangel Michael and the dedication was of Norman origin and linked to Mont- Sainte- Michel, in France. A more substantial building was erected in 1629 with seating for nearly 400. A new church was built in 1770, on land that is now at the southern end of one of Crosby's largest car parks, adjacent to Church Road. This seems to have been rather poorly built and suffered from many leaks and other faults. It survived, just, until the opening of St. Luke's in 1854. This site was later used for the St. Luke's Boys School. This building used materials from the old chapel, including some stained glass windows. Some of these bricks were used third hand to build a seat in St. Luke's churchyard, which is still there today. As part of the road widening and refurbishment of the village centre in 1986 the cross was moved some fifty yards northwards to where it stands today.

From about 1708, at considerable risk to themselves, the Catholic population met for services in the priest's house in Little Crosby village. Overcrowding soon forced the construction in 1719, of a temporary church building called West Lane Chapel, opposite the site of the present primary school. With the easing of restrictions on the Catholic Church by the early nineteenth century, a church was built in Great Crosby dedicated to St Peter and Paul. St. Mary's Church, Little Crosby, replaced the West Lane Chapel in 1847.

As the population of Great Crosby spread into Blundellsands, seawards from College Road, along Moor Lane and southwards towards Brownmoor Lane, certain amenities had to follow. To Victorian society this meant churches, then schools. Shops, including inns, would naturally follow, but amenities for entertainment were rarely considered. The Non-Conformist movement rose up during the eighteenth century. The first church to be established to the north of Liverpool was the Waterloo Congregational Church based at their chapel in East Street, in 1840.

For many centuries most education had been the business of the church. Its aim was to teach children the gospel message, and for the elite few, a sufficient level of literacy to read the Bible in Latin and, much later, in English. The labouring class, which was by far the majority, considered that boys were for working, and girls for looking after the home and rearing children. You didn't need to read or add up to achieve these aims. This attitude lasted until well into the nineteenth century; there was no overall government responsibility for education in Britain until 1870.

ST. LUKE'S CHURCH

By 1668 a parsonage was needed for the increasing needs of the parishioners of Great Crosby. It was built on land to the south of the Liverpool Road/Moor Lane junction. It later became a farm house. In spite of the demands for it to be turned into a Museum of Crosby by Charles Lamb, the author of the book 'Story of Crosby', it was demolished in 1936. The premises of Humphreys the funeral directors now occupy this site. By the 1760s the chapel of St. Michael was causing great concern because of faults in the structure.

In 1769 the decision was taken to demolish the building and replace it with a new, brick-built church. The cost of the land and building however came to £1,056 17s, less £40 for the small amount of recyclable materials. This sum of money was far beyond the means of Great Crosby's tenant farmers so an appeal was made and money was collected from as far away as Chester and York. The new church was opened in 1770

The church of St Michael in Crosby village was in a very sorry state of repair by 1850, but by then the funds were available to start the new building on the new site next to the parsonage in Liverpool Road. It was built in the Gothic style of Upholland stone, at a cost of £3,500. The dedication to an overtly Catholic saint was not considered very politic for the local parish church, so a change was indicated. The feast day of St Michael of Monte Tumba was 16th October. To cause minimum disruption the nearest alternative was chosen. This was 18th October, the feast of St. Luke.

The cost was borne by voluntary subscription and generous donations from the some of the new wealthier arrivals in the town. One

LEFT St. Luke's churchyard seat from materials used in old St. Michael's church and the Church Boys School, Crosby Village.

of the benefactors, John Myers of Crosby House, laid the foundation stone in 1853 and the church was consecrated on 26th December as the parish church of Great Crosby. Great Crosby became a separate parish in its own right, based on the church of St. Luke's on the 29th October 1875. The old church building in the village was then demolished, except for the square brick tower. This was kept as an observatory and look out for the people of Crosby. Unfortunately the ceiling and part of the roof of the main building had collapsed; it was a brave soul who climbed the stairs to the tower roof. The tower was demolished in 1880. St. Luke's is still the only Protestant church burial ground in Crosby. The opening of the Garden of Rest in Thornton in 1939 alleviated pressure on land for burial. St. Luke's suffered a very damaging fire in 1972, but is now fully restored.

ST. NICHOLAS CHURCH

In the 1840s the population of Brighton-le-sands, then called Little Brighton, was 190. Of these 57 were classed as illiterate child labourers. The Corder family had a presence in the Warrenhouse Road area. Mrs. Corder lived in a cottage in Green Lane; her family owned a general shop at No. 11 Warrenhouse for many years. She took pity on these children and felt the need to teach them to read and tell them the gospel story. Mrs. Corder held meetings in her cottage on Thursday evenings and the occasional Sunday. The

number of children coming to her meetings rapidly outgrew her little school, now dedicated to St. Barnabas. With the help of many in the area, and beyond, she managed to raise enough money to purchase a plot of land close to her cottage, fronting on to Warrenhouse Road opposite the Royal Oak and next door to the Ship Inn. It would appear that her evangelical zeal extended to the local drinkers as well as their children! The cost of building a school came to £350 – raised once more from some local people, other congregations in the Crosby area who recognised the good work that she was doing, and the benevolence of the only wealthy resident of Brighton-le-sands, Mr. Richard Houghton of Sandheys. The building was finished in 1855 and opened in January 1856. Mrs. Corder then handed over the reins to another local lady, Mrs. Eccles of Ivy Cottage. From 1862 what was now in effect a church was serviced by visiting preachers from all over the Crosby area. A need was now recognised for an Anglican church for the Blundellsands area. The licence was obtained in 1864 and a temporary iron building, dedicated to St. Barnabas, was erected on the sand dunes between Agnes Road and Warren Road at a cost of £956 14s 1d. The original building in Warrenhouse Road became the church school, and is now the Crosby Kindergarten. The iron church was opened on 14th August 1870 and attracted many of the new, wealthy residents of the area. The sight of such luminaries as the

*ABOVE St. Barnabas tin church 1870–1874. Replaced by St. Nicholas church.
Mersey Road is to the right leading to the original level crossing.*

Mellors family of wine merchants, Joseph Gardner the timber merchant and William (later Sir William) Forwood, all cramming into a prefabricated metal structure for Sunday worship was not going to last long. Even as the iron church was opened plans were well advanced for the construction of a permanent stone building on the corner of Mersey Road and Bridge Road. The Lord Bishop of Chester formally opened this church, dedicated to St. Nicholas, on 25th September 1874. The church hall was added in 1906 and extended in 1957. The temporary iron church was dismantled and an imposing vicarage built on the site. This building is now an Abbeyfield rest home. The house attached to the vicarage was formerly a private house, now a rest home, but has retained the name 'Cairn Dhu'. In 1959 a

new vicarage was built adjacent to the more modern church school in Nicholas Road.

From 1895 to 1952 a mission hall, covered by members of St. Nicholas church, was established in Brighton Road. This road, off College Road, changed its name to Jubilee Road in 1935 to celebrate King George V's 25 years on the throne.

ALL SAINTS, FOREFIELD LANE

As the population of the Brownmoor Lane, Forefield Lane, Chesterfield Road Area increased there was a need for a place of Anglican worship. In 1911 the Liverpool timber merchant Joseph Gardner, who lived at Uplands on Burbo Bank Road, gave land in Forefield Lane for a new church and efforts were made to raise the necessary funds for a building. It took 23 years, until 3rd June 1934 before a temporary hut was obtained and erected. The biggest problem was access to the church. Forefield Lane and Brownmoor Lane were unlit muddy tracks. The foundation stone for a brick built church hall was laid on 1st November 1934 and the building was opened in April 1935. The present church dates from 1957 although the original hall is still in use.

ST. MICHAEL'S, BLUNDELLSANDS

The Methodists erected a temporary metal church on the corner of Bridge Road and Mersey Road, in 1879. Known as the 'Tin Tabernacle', this was dismantled and offered by its owner Joseph Gardner to the parish of St. Luke's as a mission plant in the Blundellsands area. It was rebuilt on the site of the present church hall in Dowhills Road

and was consecrated in 1907 as the church of St. Michael in memory of the original chapel. This selfless act considerably reduced the income of St. Luke's as many of their wealthiest patrons moved to the new church. The parish of St. Michael, consisting of parts of the parishes of Sefton and St. Luke's, was recognised in June 1924. The present building was consecrated on 20th May 1931. The old tin church was used as a church hall until the present one was built in 1962. A small wooden extension of the tin church still exists in the church grounds.

ST. FAITH'S

Although called St. Faith's, Great Crosby, this church is in Waterloo. The Archbishop of York consecrated the building on 21st April 1900

RIGHT Last vestige of the old St. Michael's church, Blundellsands.

ABOVE St. Peter and Paul's church 1823–1894.

ST. PETER AND PAUL'S ROMAN CATHOLIC CHURCH

Some mission work based in Little Crosby was in evidence in Great Crosby from the mid-1700s. The first church was built in 1823, just south of the present building on Liverpool Road. Growth of the population over the ensuing sixty years showed up the inadequacy of this building. It was demolished and replaced with the present, larger building in 1894.

To the rear of the church is a small burial ground. One of the more imposing memorials is to the Coury family. Raphael Coury, a refugee of apparently Lebanese origin set up as a general merchant in Liverpool in the 1880s and became successful enough to buy a large house in Waterloo Park. His son, Gabriel George Coury was born in 1898 and volunteered for King and Country in 1914. As a second lieutenant in the Prince of Wales Volunteers, the Third Battalion South Lancashire Regiment it is possible that he did

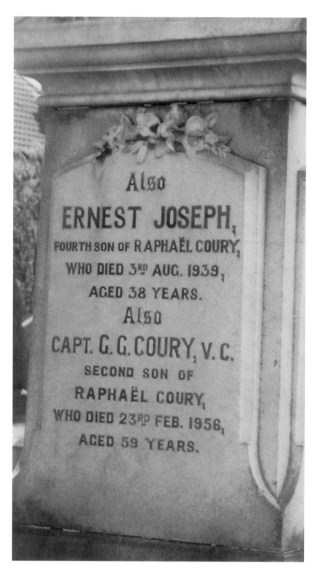

ABOVE Tomb of Gabriel Coury V.C. St. Peter and Paul's Church.

some of his initial training at the Drill Hall in Coronation Road. This building is now the Crosby Youth Centre. His battalion was dispatched to the Somme in July 1916 and on 8th August he rescued several of his men whilst under heavy enemy fire at Arrow Head Copse. For this he was awarded Crosby's only Victoria Cross. He survived the dreadful battles of the Somme but decided, not surprisingly, that trench warfare was not for him, and enlisted in the Royal Flying Corps. Coury survived the war and died in 1956.

ST. HELEN'S CHURCH, CROSBY

By the 1920s SS Peter and Paul's Church was becoming overcrowded. The need was realised for a new building in Crosby Village. A site next to St. Michael's Well and the Village Green was purchased in 1926 and a new church was built. It was officially opened on September 14th 1930. By the 1950s this building was proving inadequate and there were problems with its structure. There were long term plans for road widening and redevelopment of the area which led to the planning of a new and more modern building on the site to accommodate up to 400 people. This was opened in 1973.

ST. JOSEPH'S ROMAN CATHOLIC CHURCH, BLUNDELLSANDS

After the successful clearing and drainage of area we know as Blundellsands, Nicholas Blundell was planning an exclusive development of fine houses for the new rich Liverpool merchants. Apart from the houses themselves a church was essential. A site, among the sand dunes, on the corner of Warren Road and the Serpentine, was reserved on 14th February 1880. Because of the financial demands of the proposed Roman Catholic cathedral in Liverpool, work did not start until 1885. Until the building was opened, in November 1886, the Catholics in the Blundellsands area were happy to walk or ride to SS Peter and Paul's or to St. Mary's, Little Crosby. With the completion of the

Presbytery, in 1890, there was room for a congregation of 400. This may seem excessive but the lesson of population growth had been learnt from the initial inadequacy of SS Peter and Paul's. There was also a large number of domestic servants employed in Blundellsands, mostly Irish.

METHODISTS

Methodists met in each other's houses until 1863 when a site near the corner of Liverpool Road and Moor Lane was identified for a meeting place. This grand, ornate chapel and a church hall were opened in July 1863. In 1879, with the growth of the Blundellsands

RIGHT Line drawing of St. Helen's church, Crosby Village 1930–1972.

area a temporary metal structure, the 'Tin Tabernacle' was erected on the corner of Bridge Road and Mariners Road, a site later occupied by a branch of Barclay's bank. The increase in the size of the congregation forced the search for a much larger site. This was found in Mersey Road in the late 1880s. It was decided to demolish the chapel in Liverpool Road and use the materials towards the building of a church on this prime site.

The chapel was pulled down in 1890 and the new church opened in September. Many of the Liverpool Road congregation were unhappy with this decision and continued to meet in the church hall until its closure in December 2001. The front part of the building was used as the Crossroads Centre from 1988 until the centre moved to new purpose built premises, in September 2003. The Mersey Road church was considered sufficient for the needs of

RIGHT Wesleyan chapel,
Liverpool Road
1863–1890.

Crosby's congregation, and, in 1907, the 'Tin Tabernacle' was passed on to the Anglican Church for the site in Dowhills Road. The church hall was used as a rest and reception centre during the blitz, and was badly damaged in an air raid on 13th March 1941. In 1990 preparations were well under way for a weekend of celebrations to mark the church's centenary. The Friday before, the 28th September, the church was badly damaged by fire. It has been rebuilt but without its impressive spire.

A small gathering of Methodists from the Moor Lane area had been meeting in the Old Farm House in Chesterfield Road. In 1935 a site was obtained in Moor Lane nearly opposite the windmill. Moor Lane Methodist Church was opened in 1937. The current and much larger building dates from 1959. The original one became the church hall.

A group of Independent Methodists had been meeting in accommodation that was built in 1910 as a public house, which had failed to obtain the necessary licence. This stood on the corner of Endbutt Lane and Musker Street. Land was obtained in Seafield Avenue and the foundation stone for a chapel was laid in July 1914. The First World War interrupted the construction, but it was finally completed in 1920. An alcohol licence was granted for the original building but it was in a very poor state and was demolished in the early 1920s. The Endbutt Hotel took over the licence and the present building of 1924 now stands on the site.

CONGREGATIONALISTS

As early as 1844 the Liverpool Congregational Building Society secured a site in Eshe Road for Crosby's growing number of Congregationalists. The site was purchased in 1861, and a building was erected in 1882 at a cost of £710. This became the church hall and Sunday school when the main church was built and opened in 1897. In 1972 the Congregational Church joined with the English Presbyterians to form the United Reformed Church.

PRESBYTERIANS

Presbyterians in Crosby met in various houses until November 1897. The group was then big enough to rent a room in the Assembly Rooms (later Alexandra Hall). In March 1898 yet another of the ubiquitous temporary metal churches was built at the rear of the Blundellsands Hotel, on the site of what became the Hotel ballroom. This was enlarged several times until 1905, when the building of a church commenced on the corner of Warren Road and the Serpentine, opposite the Roman Catholic church of St. Joseph. The church hall was added in 1928, but was destroyed during the 1941 May blitz. This incident, on the night of 4th May, also blew out most of the church's stained glass windows. A new hall was built in 1952. This church became part of the United Reform Church in 1972.

CHAPTER 4
LEARNING

During the Middle Ages education in Crosby was invariably organised by the church. The priests at Sefton church tried to spot those sons of farmers who could be trained for the priesthood. The teaching was very rudimentary, limited to basic reading, writing and religious instruction. Almost from its foundation the chapel of St. Michael felt a responsibility to encourage some of the young people to look beyond the family small holding for their future. Not surprisingly this did not always find favour among some of the parents of these boys, the agricultural workers that made up almost all of Great Crosby's population. After all you did not need to read and write to work a plough, dig ditches or tend sheep. Nor did the girls need these skills for spinning cooking or brewing. Although decreasing, this attitude prevailed well into the late 1800s. Children were not required to read and write to clean chimneys or work down coal mines.

Eventually more of Crosby's farmers could see the advantages of an education that could enhance the quality of life of their children. Several of the families began to buy up land throughout the area, increasing their holdings as well as their flocks and grazing land. Amongst these newly aspiring middle classes were the Harrison family. Their original farm was probably along Moor Lane, and they became, very rich; nowhere near the wealth of the Blundells and the Molyneuxs of course,

but certainly by the standards prevailing in the fields and marshes of sixteenth century Great Crosby.

Many of the merchants scouring the country looking for the best wool would have visited the Harrison lands. John Harrison would have heard the tales they told of the vast wealth of the cloth tycoons of Antwerp and Ypres, and the fact that London was becoming more and more the centre of this trade. He visited the wool fairs of Lancashire and made many contacts and gathered much useful information about the trade that would one day make him a very rich man. The young John Harrison left Crosby in 1555 to seek his fortune in London. In spite of this Dick Whittington act he did not become Lord Mayor, but eventually became a member of the Merchant Taylor's Guild, one of the city's twelve great livery companies. When the Reformation made the overtly religious nature of the guilds difficult to uphold many of the rich merchants diversified into education. Some had already endowed schools in their home towns; a free grammar school had been established in London in 1561. John Harrison died in 1592 a very wealthy man. He left money to many of his relatives in Crosby and did not forget the chapel of St. Michael. His son, also John, remembered his father's desire to endow a grammar school in Crosby. John junior visited the town for the first time in

1617. He was dismayed to find it a poor place with very little communication with the outside world. At the time of the visit Great Crosby was still a huddle of rough cottages centred round a small chapel in need of repair, and a total population of less than six hundred. He could see little potential in the village itself and any other pupils would have the long walk over the sand dunes from Liverpool, or along the hazardous tracks from Thornton or Sefton. Nor could he have anticipated the growth of the port of Liverpool. However his father had allowed for the endowment of a school so a suitable piece of land was eventually purchased on the track leading south of the village towards Liverpool. The school was built and opened, for boys only, by 1622 with a master (at £30 per annum) and an usher – assistant master, (at £20 per annum). This building, with its many extensions, is now the oldest in the township. The school suffered many ups and downs over the next couple of centuries, but many of the pupils went on to make distinguished careers in commerce, the church, higher education, government and the diplomatic service. At times Merchant Taylor's School nearly closed down through lack of staff and pupils. Its lowest point was reached in 1848 when the roll consisted of just four pupils. Even worse these were the headmaster's children and worse again three were girls, contrary to the Merchant Taylor's company rules. As transport links improved the school increased dramatically in numbers to the extent that a new, larger building was required. The large site on the corner of Liverpool Road and what was to become College Road was purchased and the construction started in 1872. The new school was opened by the Countess of Derby in 1878 as the most imposing building in Great Crosby. It still is and is well known as a landmark and many directions are given to visitors based on its easily recognisable clock tower. The original building was extended, refurbished, and opened as a Girls Grammar School in 1888. To keep the fees at a reasonable level and to improve the school in line with recent developments, especially in the sciences, it was decided to accept government assistance, and the school severed its financial links with the Merchant Taylor's Guild in 1910.

A preparatory school, always known as Miss Milton's was established next to the school at 184 Liverpool Road in 1923. This department was moved to the house called Stanfield in 1973.

The Rev. Anthony Halsall was born on the Isle of Man and had many friends in the Liverpool area. He was Head of Merchant Taylor's School from 1730 to 1755. His sister Catherine moved to Crosby with him and had a strong desire to establish a school to teach the girls of the village basic reading and writing as well as knitting and sewing. Catherine Halsall died in 1758 and left sufficient funds in her will to purchase a property and set it up as one of the first girl's schools in the country. Known originally as the Girls School and then the

Mistress School it eventually became Halsall School. The site for the school, as provided for in Catherine Halsall's will, was a plot of land known as Thorpe's Tenement in Cooks Road. It ceased to be a totally private venture in 1851 and became connected to the parish of St. Luke. A new building was erected on the site in 1912. In 1946 this was considered totally inadequate and in very poor condition. It took 28 years to make a firm decision to demolish this out dated building and build a new one on the site. At the last minute it was decided to build an extension instead. This was finally opened in March 1977.

The National Society for the Education of the Poor was founded in 1811 by the Church of England in an attempt to provide basic free education with a consistent curriculum through-out the country. These became known as 'National schools'. One was established on what is now the front garden of St. Luke's church, in about 1822. It had separate boys and girls departments. This building was in very poor condition by the late 1860s so was pulled down about 1870. The old Crosby village chapel had been demolished in 1852 (apart from the tower) and the site, and some of the material, including the stained glass windows, was used to build the Great Crosby C of E School for boys on the chapel site. Material from the demolished National school was also used. Recycling is not that new! This was opened on 30th January 1871 and served the young men of Crosby until it was cleared in 1974 to make way for the car park in Church

Road. During the Second World War the school was often taken over for military use and at one time the headmaster was given the title 'Local organizer for the gathering of blackberries by school children' – surely a unique honour. The girls were sent to the Halsall School. The other Church of England primary school was the one attached to St. Nicholas' church, in Warrenhouse Road. By the late 1950s this became totally inadequate for the needs of the area and funds became available for building an entirely new school on the so called 'Buttercup Fields', in Nicholas Road. This was completed in late 1961 and the move of equipment and pupils began in November. The new school was up and running by the spring of 1962.

Between the Reformation and the general emancipation in the 1830s, education of Roman Catholic children was essentially of a clandestine nature. The first school for Catholic children was built by William Blundell in 1842 and was opened in November 1843. This was right on the boundary between Great and Little Crosby by the bridge over Thornback Pool. The building is still there and is now a private residence called 'Boundary Cottage'. With the opening of the church school of SS Peter and Paul's (now known as Great Crosby Catholic Primary School), and the village school of St. Mary's in Little Crosby, this school became redundant and closed in 1859. It was taken over by Nicholas Blundell as a base for some of the local men who had been organized into a company of yeoman of the Second Division of Lancashire Volunteer Artillery. It was defended (against who – the recalcitrant farmers of Great Crosby perhaps?), by four muzzle loading cannons of doubtful vintage, with a neat stack of cannon balls at the ready. In 1867 it became the dwelling house it now is.

After the First World War families were getting smaller as was the number of domestic staff. Many of the houses in the area were too large for the families that occupied them. For many of these houses the progression to flats and then nursing homes started with their conversion to private schools. Several of these were the so-called 'dame schools'. The ravages of the trenches left many unmarried ladies with very small incomes, if any at all. They banded together in groups of twos and threes, bought up the large houses and set up schools. The standard of teaching in these schools was very patchy. Some were very good, and a number of them survived into the 1960s. Streatham House, in Victoria Road, founded in 1925, and Atherton House, survive today with excellent records. Atherton House started as a private venture in various houses in 1937 but found a permanent home in Alexandra Road in 1949. Some however were very poor and did not last for long even without Ofsted reports. In 1931 the Ursuline Sisters set up a convent school in Blundellsands. Four large houses were bought, Overdale, Seathwaite, St. Olave's and Inveralt. Two were used as the primary school and one for a nursery. The remaining building was demolished and the site used for playing fields... This became a voluntary aided Catholic primary school in 1968.

New local authority county primary schools were established in Forefield Lane (1937), Vale Road (1961), and Sherwood Avenue (1971). Falling rolls in the 1980s saw an amalgamation in September 1984, of Vale school (which had moved to the empty Coronation Road County Secondary School in 1974) and Sherwood Avenue at the Sherwood site, to be named Valewood. The old Coronation Road building was demolished to make way for 'Sandalwood' retirement flats. Vale School in St. Luke's Road was taken over by another amalgamation, that of two special schools, Menai Court and Rowan Park.

Before the introduction of comprehensive education any child who passed the 'eleven plus' examination became eligible for entrance to a grammar school. If he or she wished to stay in Crosby the only choice was between the Catholic schools or those in the independent sector. As well as Merchant Taylor's there was the option of St. Mary's College, or, for a short time, Blundellsands House School.

Edmund Rice formed the Order of Christian Brothers of Ireland in 1820. They established several schools in Ireland before moving over the Irish Sea. They were asked to set up a school in Crosby in 1914. The war held up progress but negotiations were opened for the purchase of Claremont House in Liverpool Road. This was the former home of the United States consul in Liverpool and was established as the Catholic Institute in September 1919. A site was acquired in Everest Road and the purpose built St. Mary's College was built. It opened in 1924 and Claremont House became the preparatory school.

The Religious Order of the Sacred Heart of Mary was founded in France in 1848. A presence in the Bootle area was established in 1872, whereupon the quest was on for suitable premises to start a school. Seafield House in Seaforth was about to be turned into a luxury hotel but for financial reasons it never opened as such. The building was taken over by the order in 1880. With the expansion northwards of the Liverpool docks the building was sold to the Mersey Docks and Harbour Board in 1905, and the nuns moved to temporary accommodation in a large house in Kimberley Drive, whilst the imposing building in Liverpool Road was completed. The school, eventually to be known as Seafield Catholic Grammar School for Girls, was opened in 1908. A preparatory school was added at The Villas, next door in 1927 and boys were accepted from 1972.

The Catholic secondary modern school, St. Bede's, opened in 1961 in Myers Road East, amalgamated with Seafield in 1977, and so Sacred Heart Comprehensive was born.

Waterloo High School was established as a private secondary school in 1865 with premises in Hyde Road, Waterloo. The school moved to Oxford Road in 1873 and, in 1888, bought the large property Blundellsands House in Burbo Bank Road South. It was advertised as a 'private boarding and day school for young gentlemen'. The school

playing fields were on one half of Rossett Park – the other half being used by Marine F.C. The name changed to Blundellsands School in 1913 and Blundellsands House School in 1923. It closed in 1930. Soon after, the playing fields were sold and used for the Crosender Road housing development.

The main non-Catholic secondary modern school was Coronation Road County Secondary established in 1912. In the 1950s a decision was made to change this school's status from co-educational to boys only. A school for girls was built on the corner of Manor Road and St. Michael's Road and the first intake of girls (from Coronation Road) arrived in September 1955. It was officially opened in April 1956.

The start of the school year in September 1972 saw a huge upheaval in education in the borough. Comprehensive education had been a political football for several years but that year saw it arrive in Crosby – not without problems.

Manor Road Secondary School for Girls, Waterloo Grammar, and Crosby County Secondary, Crosby Road North, became Manor High School, based on the buildings of the girl's school in Manor Road.

A site in Chesterfield Road had been identified for a possible replacement for the Coronation Road School. With the coming of comprehensive education Coronation Road County Secondary School and Waterloo Park Grammar School for Girls became Chesterfield High School.

CHAPTER 5
TRAVELLING

The farmers of Great Crosby, in common with those of most of the country, had no desire or reason to travel far. The economy of those early times only required their land to produce enough food for their families, and a little over to pay in rent or taxes. Their only real journey was to church on Sunday. For this they used the track from Crosby Village, along what is now Moor Lane to head for the beacon of the spire of St. Helen's church. This track was very often unsuitable for wheeled vehicles, especially the carriage of coffins to the church graveyard.

In 1324 Edward II visited the then very small port of Liverpool. When proceeding northwards he found the roads so bad that he had to resort to being carried on a litter. This was only used when other methods were impossible.

From the foundation of the house of Tudor, in 1485, Britain gained the benefits of a strong, relatively stable, central government. Economic growth increased and with it more traffic, though there was very little evidence in the Crosby area. The first stirrings of an industrial society in Lancashire proved that the production of goods was useless without the means of distribution. In many areas road maintenance was a monastic duty. Henry VIII's dissolution of the monasteries effectively stopped this, but ultimately led to the passing of the 1555 Highways Act. This provided unpaid labour to keep the local road system in some semblance of order. Every parishioner had to spend four days a year working unpaid, on road repair. Naturally when it was the turn of the richer parishioners they would pay the poor peasants to do their share. This was extended to six days in 1563.

In spite of this Act the roads around Crosby were in very poor condition. Transport to Liverpool or Ormskirk was impassable most of the year to wheeled traffic and in winter it was very difficult to ride or walk. Nicholas Blundell's diaries are full of accounts of the problems of travelling even the short journey between Great and Little Crosby in winter. The preferred way to travel from Crosby to Liverpool, or northwards, was along the sands (subject to the tide of course). This was not a perfect surface and many accidents were caused by the overturning of coaches and wagons. In spite of the difficulties a regular coach run was established in 1754. The regularity of this service became somewhat erratic depending on the weather and sand conditions. There was an alternative should you wish to travel further a field, to Ireland for instance. In the early eighteenth century it was possible to stand on the beach at Crosby and wave a handkerchief at a passing ship. Should weather conditions be right, and if the captain was so inclined, a small boat would put out to the shore and pick you up. One has to assume that this was not a common occurrence. By 1700 there were regulations in place about the track width of vehicles, and therefore of the roads, and also concerning signposts and their maintenance. It is doubtful however whether any of these were enforced with any regularity. There is evidence that during the seventeenth and early eighteenth centuries the climate changed. One of the results was a significant increase in rainfall. This made the jobs of road repairers and travellers even more difficult. Also the unpaid labourers were beginning to get angry about regularly filling in holes and removing mud, not for local people but for passing traffic. This passing trade contributed nothing to local funds. This same problem reared its head with the arrival of the motor car 200 years later. There was only one answer. Whoever used any section of road must pay towards its maintenance. So the Turnpike system arrived around 1706. A toll was exacted depending on the size and weight of the vehicle, and often at the whim of the gate keeper. The nearest to Crosby was that between Liverpool and Preston The Turnpike trusts were the beginning of a basically sound road system, although they were eventually killed off by the railways. By 1800 the roads everywhere, even in outlying areas like Crosby, were improving to the point where passenger traffic was becoming profitable. Although the turnpike system was virtually at an end by 1840, there was a proposal to build one linking the rising seaside resorts of Waterloo and Brighton (le sands). This was to start from the junction of York Street and Great Georges Road. It would then proceed along Mount Pleasant, Oxford Road (then called Brighton Road), and Mersey View (then called Little Brighton). The plan came too late – the railway had arrived. The railway was seen as fast, low maintenance, and therefore profitable. The spread of the railway system killed off the lucrative stage coach trade, and the roads began to deteriorate again. This did not apply to the urban areas where even the lower paid began to travel outside their immediate confines, and use the horse bus for local travel.

In 1830 Samuel Towers, the proprietor of the Royal Hotel started a horse bus service for the people of Bootle and North Liverpool to come and enjoy the beaches of Waterloo. Within four years the service was extended to Crosby Village and provided four trips a day. By 1840 this became an hourly service. He was bought out by the Liverpool Omnibus Conveyancing Company in 1860. This year also saw Birkenhead introducing the very first horse buses on rails. In 1879 the Liverpool United Tramway and Omnibus Company bought out all existing rival companies and reduced the service to ten a day. The advantages of horses pulling buses on rails were less dependence on state of road surface, and less friction between metal wheels and track. This meant that each horse could pull a bigger load, therefore more passengers, therefore more profit. Liverpool Corporation became responsible for the service, in 1897.

Various experiments had been tried to substitute electric power for horse power. The use of a third, live rail in the street from which the current could be picked up was a possibility, but, fortunately for Crosby's pedestrians it was never seriously considered. One hates to think of the resultant death toll! The overhead wire was the obvious route. Various cities introduced this system during the 1890s. A Bill of 1899 allowed the Liverpool Overhead Railway and Liverpool Corporation to construct a tramway system into Crosby. Work commenced in September 1899 on a single track from the Seaforth Sands depot of the Overhead Railway to the terminus at the junction of Victoria Road and Cooks Road.

After several successful trial runs from Seaforth to Five Lamps (Great Georges Road), the extension to the Crosby terminus had thirteen passing loops to enable more than one car to use the track. There were some problems with this section as the Waterloo roads were laid with square setts, those in Crosby with rectangular setts. There was also the added problem that wooden setts were used outside churches to reduce noise. A regular service was in operation by the end of 1901. Fourteen cars were obtained, of which eight were open top double-deckers. 22 passengers could be accommodated inside on long, hard, wooden benches, 28 on top with high side rails to protect passengers from the overhead wires. Two cars were single deck with accommodation for 32, 40 at a pinch. The last four were more stylish and allowed

36 on the partially covered upper deck with fancy guard rails. Two more of these, numbers 15 and 16, were purchased in 1903. The single deckers were withdrawn from service in 1914. By 1914 the trams were operating in a green and cream livery with Seaforth, Waterloo and Great Crosby painted on the sides of the upper deck. They carried advertisements on all available spaces but no route indicators or route numbers (there was after all only one). The service was run Monday to Friday every six minutes from 5 a.m. to 11 p.m., and every twelve minutes on a Sunday morning. The sixteen minute journey from Seaforth to Great Crosby cost 2d. The fare rose to 3d. in 1920.

In the early 1920s the motor bus was beginning to appear in greater numbers and the last Crosby tram was run in 1925. An attempt to introduce a bus service from Crosby station to Thornton by the Lancashire and Yorkshire Railway, in 1907, failed after a very short time.

The Waterloo and Crosby Motor Services was established in 1923 with 15 ex-London buses. These were the pre-1914 types affectionately known as 'Old Bills'. The first service started from Five Lamps and then via Crosby Road, Liverpool Road and Moor Lane to a terminus at Chestnut Avenue. This was soon extended to the Nags Head pub in Thornton, and southwards into Litherland. Norwest Bus Services took over in 1927 and operated a Southport to Liverpool service, via Crosby and Bootle. This was in turn taken over by Ribble, with an hourly service, from 1928. Ribble had a virtual monopoly of public transport on the roads of Crosby until the arrival of deregulation in 1986.

By the late 1920s the private motor car began to be an influence on the transport needs and desires of the Crosby area, as indeed the whole country. The first motor car in South Lancashire appeared on the streets of Southport in 1896. Unfortunately it is not possible to trace the first car owner in Crosby as it would have been registered at County Hall in Preston in 1903, and the pre 1921 records are lost. There must have been very few motor cars in Crosby when one considers that barely 4,000 were registered for the whole of Lancashire County Council between 1903 and 1920. Liverpool boasted a large number of premises purporting to sell and repair cars by 1900. These establishments also sold bicycles and, to hedge their bets, rented and sold carriages and livery horses. Of the garages listed here it should be remembered that they were engineering establishments who repaired cars only. Some would have been able to order new cars (there were no agencies) and occasionally sold second hand vehicles. Breakdown services were not generally available until the 1930s. Petrol was obtained in two or four gallon 'bottles' from chandlers or chemist's shops provided that they had the requisite licence. Petrol pumps, usually operating on a shilling in the slot system, only entered general use in the late 1920s.

Maitland's shop in Victoria Road, established in 1891, was granted a licence to supply petroleum spirit in 1900. A motor car repair service was established by Leonard Myerscough at 7 Liverpool Road in 1906 and at 1 and 25 Liverpool Road in 1913. The garage at 25 Liverpool Road next to the George Hotel was formally a coach house and stables. From here, every Sunday morning a coach would run down Moor Lane to Sefton church. Alas the tale is told that the women and children used the service to go to church whilst most of the men went to the Punchbowl Inn next door to drink and engage in various games of chance. Myerscough's were also for a time at 3 Moor Lane, the present site of the Age Concern shop. This was the home of various bicycle shops until it became Weir's Garage in 1937. Weir's closed in 1961 when the building became a bank.

The engineering company of Bramhall and Robinson set up Robinson's Crosby Park Garage in 1913. This became the College Motor Company in 1918. They traded from this site until 1964 then moved to 26 Bridge Road, Brighton-le –sands. Cain's, the filling station occupied the site until 1971. Crosby Park Garage as it now is was formed in 1973.

T. Gibson's Motor Company, College Road was established opposite Alexandra Road in 1913. It ceased trading in 1923.

The 1920s saw a rapid increase in the number of vehicles on the roads. With this came the rise of establishments to deal with all aspects of servicing the new activity of motoring.

Armour and Webster's Claremount Motor Garage was established in Claremount Road in 1923, as was Kelly's Garage in Bridge Road. Kelly's moved further along Oxford Road in 1924 and was replaced by Hepburn's Garage, which continued in business until 2002. A gentleman with the wonderful name of Hector Macdonald Chipchase opened his garage on the corner of Coronation Road and Islington in 1924. He barely lasted two years. Other well-known establishments were Livock and Edwards opening in 1926, Crown Motor Works at 42 Liverpool Road in1928, Frodsham's and Alexandra Garage, College Road, the site of present filling station, in about 1926, having moved from Mersey Road (what is now the Delta Garage). Also flourishing were J.W.Stansfield's, at the Serpentine (attached to Blundellsands Hotel), and Rigbys then Finnegans in Coronation Road next to Crosby Park Garage.

Smith and Gardners opened up a car sales business in Allengate, off Moor Lane in 1964. When the area was cleared for car parking in the late 1970s the business was transferred to Coronation Road. They also used the Delta garage site in Mersey Road. Smith and Gardners ceased trading in 1988.

William Henry Harrington founded stables for livery horses in Liverpool in the late 1850s. The premises were first recorded in Parliament Street in 1860 and then in Queen Anne Street in 1862. By then he was building and repairing carriages and involved in the lucrative weddings and funerals business. He moved into Crosby in 1898 establishing his business at 1 Agnes Road. The funeral side of the business

ABOVE Harrington's original sign on Sunnyside House. Note the telephone number Crosby 11.

operated from Moor Lane adjacent to the old George Inn, in 1905, and within two or three years Harrington's was established at several addresses in the Liverpool Road part of the village. He became so successful that he bought the house Sunnyside on Mersey Road bridge and the large adjacent area (now the Delta garage) in 1909. William Harrington himself lived in Harlech Road.

Ben Lloyd opened a cycle shop in College Road in 1910. He moved to Bridge Road in 1914 and soon extended his interest to motor cycles. This shop is still there although recently renamed Bridge Motor Cycles.

Geneva Motors, 70 Coronation Road sold motor cycles up until 1965. These premises are now occupied by the Liver Laundrette.

CANALS

There was one method of travel which had been used for centuries. Britain is blessed with a network of navigable rivers. They were free and needed very little adoption by man. Unfortunately they did not always go to the places that you, or your goods, wanted to go.

The idea of connecting rivers with man made waterways, or even carving them out of land where no rivers ran, was considered in the 1500s. It was not until the mid-1700s that the level of civil engineering expertise was available and what became known as the time of 'canal-mania' gripped the country. One of the most ambitious schemes was the trans-Pennine Leeds and Liverpool canal. This was first surveyed in 1767 and construction started in 1775. This began with the easy bit – Liverpool to Wigan, opened the following year. Although primarily designed to carry coal from collieries in the Wigan area, the potential for passengers and mail soon became apparent. From 1824 a canal boat called the 'Lancashire Witch' carried passengers at a sedate 6 miles per hour through the countryside from Liverpool to Bootle and Crosby. These boats were hauled by two horses in tandem and a postilion rode one sounding his horn to warn of the boats coming and to tell the passengers when the next stopping place was near. By 1845 there were five trips a day increasing to seven on fine summer days. One could be met at the Crosby stop and take a carriage up to the sea shore. All this for a penny a mile or 1?d for a seat. The coming of the railway quickly killed off the passenger canal service.

RAILWAYS

The steam locomotive became a reliable and safe form of transport in the 1830s. The building of railways spread throughout the country. Driven by the ruthless attitude of the engineers who saw every obstacle, natural or man-made, as a challenge; and by the financial pressure of the railway barons and their share-holders, no beauty spot or historic site was safe. Well not many. In the mid-1840s there was a plan to link Liverpool and Southport with branches to Ormskirk and other parts of south west Lancashire. The track would go through Great Crosby and Little Crosby. The Blundell family however had other ideas. They had gone to considerable trouble to preserve their way of life, free from the smoke and dirt of progressive technology. So they offered a financial incentive. The area known as Blundellsands, largely owned by the family, was attracting new money from the port of Liverpool. It therefore made sense to the Blundells to route the railway along the seashore side of Crosby. The sandhills area on which they proposed that the railway should run was given to the company free of charge.

The first sod on the single track railway from Waterloo to Southport was cut on the 24th March 1848 and the line was officially opened on 21st July. According to William Forwood, the first journey was by horse drawn 'carriages'. The VIPs were not to be

ABOVE Original station house, Mersey Road.

covered with coal dust! The Liverpool, Crosby and Southport Railway service began on the 24th, four months to the day between the first spade cut to an operating railway! Initially five trains a day were provided, linking with the horse bus services from Liverpool to Waterloo. The third class single fare was one shilling. These passengers stood in open trucks with sides high enough to preclude any view but not high enough to keep away the steam and coal dust. Two shillings bought a second class ticket which provided wooden bench seats and sides low enough to see the view. For two shillings and sixpence (12?p), you got padded upholstered seats.

Stopping places at Crosby and Ainsdale were soon established and, and, in 1850, the line was extended southwards to Sandhills. Considerable increase in traffic saw the need for a double track. This was constructed in 1852 but it became necessary to extend the station buildings south of the Blundellsands Road level crossing. By 1855 when the Lancashire and Yorkshire railway took over the service, there were 36 trains a day. Many of these were express services stopping only at Birkdale and occasionally Formby. The spread of the desirable residences northwards provided an opportunity to open a station at Hall Road, in 1874. An extra service from

Liverpool to Hall Road was laid on. To turn the trains round as well as the need for a maintenance facility is evidence in the number of sheds and sidings at this station.

1878 saw the closing of the Blundellsands Road level crossing and the construction of the present subway, as well as Mersey Road with its bridge over the railway. Three years later the present station was built. It was about this time that the name of the station was changed to Blundellsands and Crosby.

An increase in use was soon made by the local farmers. In fact the line became known as the 'Farmers Line'. Large quantities of produce, barley, milk, vegetables, even cut flowers went to Liverpool. Also oats and hay for feeding and bedding the estimated 16,000 horses used in the city by the haulage trade. On the return journey came the manure produced by these animals for excellent fertilizer. If one intended to travel by train from Liverpool to Crosby, it would have paid to check on whether or not it was the farmer's train, and which way the wind was blowing.

In 1903 the Liverpool to Southport became the first main line track in the country to be electrified. No smoking areas were introduced – prohibited at the Southport end of each carriage, permitted at the Liverpool end.

The 27th July 1905 was a black day in the history of Crosby. The Liverpool to Hall Road suburban train had just been shunted into a siding when the 6.30 express from Liverpool to Southport, which would only have stopped at Formby and Birkdale, came through the station. It appeared that the points had not been turned back from the siding and at 6.37 p.m. the express ran straight into the back of the empty, stationery suburban train. The express was popular with office and shop workers who lived in Formby and Southport and worked in the city. The first carriage took the brunt of the collision. Miraculously the driver survived, though with serious injuries. 20 passengers were killed and 4, including the driver, badly injured. This followed a similar accident at Waterloo two years before when eight passengers died. Questions were asked about the safety aspects of electrification but these two accidents were put down to 'teething troubles'.

In 1921 the Lancashire and Yorkshire Railway was taken over by the new Lancashire and North West. This became the London, Midland and Scottish (the sadly missed L.M.S), in 1923.

TELEPHONES

Alexander Graham Bell first demonstrated the practical use of the telephone in April 1876. By August 1879 the Lancashire Telephonic Exchange Company was operating equipment for the first subscribers. The Liverpool exchange was opened on 15th October 1879 in Exchange Buildings at the rear of the town hall with 40 subscribers. Telephone service was only available only during weekdays. There was no evening or week-end service. In 1886 several sub-exchanges were opened including one over a shop in South Road,

Waterloo. Until 1898 a simple numerical system was in use but the increasing number of subscribers forced the adoption of a new system using exchange names and numbers. Waterloo numbers covered an area including Litherland, Seaforth, and Crosby. The 500th subscriber was reached by about 1900 and included Great Crosby Urban District at Waterloo 61. There were no schools nor pubs listed, and very few small businesses. The Waterloo exchange moved to its present position, a large house in Crosby Road North, in 1924. The Great Crosby exchange opened in the 1930s. Operator service was in normal use until about 1950 when dial telephones were introduced. Letter codes GRE and WAT were replaced by 924 and 928, in 1966

POSTAL SERVICES

Some form of public postal service had been in use since the seventeenth century. By the mid 1700s this was mainly carried out by postboys who were notorious for their inefficiency and slowness. The improvement in the roads, the rise of the mail coach and later the railways contributed to a much improved service. The biggest problem was that charges, by weight and distance, had to be paid by the receiver. The pre-paid penny post of 1840 led to a great improvement in the services' efficiency. For smaller towns receiving houses were set up from which mail would be collected to pass on to bigger centres. This grew into the system of sub-post offices we have today, (for a while at least!). These receiving houses were often literally private houses but usually local shops. John Roughley, a saddler, had a shop in the part of Liverpool Road which was demolished to make way for the Moor Lane By-Pass. He was appointed a receiver of posts in 1847 and continued in that capacity until about 1900. Pillar boxes first appeared on the roads of Crosby in 1859. Roughley's 'post office' was replaced by a shop at 15 Moor Lane. It moved across the road to a dedicated sub-post office, complete with pillar box, next to the mock-Tudor bank at 2 Moor Lane. The next move was to Crown Buildings in 1915 where it stayed for the next seventy years. Brighton-le-sands Post office dates from about 1875, and those in College Road and by Blundellsands station from 1905.

The postmark for this area was originally 'Bootle'. This changed to Crosby in September 1955

CHAPTER 6
LIVING AND WORKING

From the very earliest times the life of the township of Great Crosby was centred around the village with its green and the well and chapel of St. Michael's. From this centre radiated several tracks. To the east, across the bracken covered moor, went the path towards the beckoning spire of Sefton church. This would one day become Moor Lane. To the south the route went towards Liverpool. In the 1500s this only went as far as Seaforth; then began the walk across the sandhills of Bootle and Kirkdale. To the north- east went the way to Crosby Hall, Little Crosby and then the township of Moorhouses and eventually Formby. Westwards towards the sea went the route used by the fisherman, shrimpers, wreckers and maybe even smugglers and led to the shore across the treacherous Crosby Marsh. This route was called Out Lane as early as the 1600s. It is now Victoria Road and Blundellsands Road. A lane straggled north from the village to the outlying farms where Manor Road now runs. There were some important later additions. A westward route to the sea, south of Out Lane, culminated in a small group of fisherman's cottages later to be called Brighton-le-sands. This became known as Thorps Lane, and now Coronation Road. Off the Liverpool road was the way across the moor to the township of Litherland. This became Endbutt Lane and increased in use with the coming of the Leeds

and Liverpool Canal. Skirting the marsh from the Liverpool road to join up with the seaward end of Thorps lane was a track called Marsh Lane, the present College Road. This outline of roads is preserved on the present town plan of Great Crosby.

THE VILLAGE

Centuries ago Great Crosby village was simply a collection of small roughly built cottages. The men and boys tended their small holdings, planted and harvested their crops, cleared drainage ditches and looked after the few cows and sheep. The women and the girls spun the wool for clothes then ground the corn and baked the bread. Every cottage had a spinning wheel and some primitive method of grinding cereals. Originally grinding the corn was very hard work, rubbing it between two heavy stones. A later device made life a lot easier. This consisted of two round stones fitted with a wooden handle so that the corn could be ground between them. By about 1200 the windmill was developed – a larger version of the hand mill for communal use. The windmill acted as a point of social interaction for the women of the scattered community. Much gossip was exchanged whilst waiting one's turn. The nearest mill for the people of Great Crosby was that owned by the Blundell family at Little Crosby. The date of this building is unknown but it was in

ABOVE Crosby windmill c.1890.

operation in 1275. Two windmills were recorded in Great Crosby by 1290; the mill in Moor Lane was not built until 1813. Possibly the first chapel was built at about the same time as the first windmill. These mills and the chapel seem to be the earliest signs of Great Crosby's independence from its neighbours Little Crosby and Sefton. The women also brewed ale. Water was plentiful but whether its source was salt marsh, marl pit or drainage ditch it was not for drinking – we have to wait until the 1880s before you could drink water from the tap. Mixing ground barley and yeast into the water made it marginally safer to drink, as well as tasting better. The basic diet of the time consisted of coarse barley bread supplemented with cheese, milk and butter and meat and vegetables when available. This was washed down with copious quantities of weak ale. Added to this diet was the abundance of 'free' eels from the sniggeries and the ubiquitous rabbit.

The stabilisation of the nation as a whole stimulated a market economy and regularized local government and taxation. Even the subsistence farmers began to have leftover produce and a market to sell it.

Just to the north of the village was the local pinfold. This was a system that had been in operation since Anglo-Saxon times. Any stray animals were placed in an enclosed area until claimed by the owner. A fee was then paid which would include a reward for the finder, the expenses of the pinfold-keeper, known as the pinder, and any damage caused whilst the animal was loose — a sort of medieval wheel-clamping. If not claimed within a year and a day the pinder could sell the animal to defray his expenses. There were sometimes conflicts over the amount owing especially in regard to the damage caused. Compromise was usually reached at the Halmcote – a sort of small claims court, which met at St. Michael's well. The pinder's cottage was built in about 1550 on what is now the corner of Alexandra Road, and demolished only in 1963. Its memory is preserved by the name of the flats built on the opposite corner – Pinfold Court.

Sheep became important, not just for food but for the wool. English wool was highly prized (it may seem obvious but the thinner the sheep, the thicker the wool – and Crosby sheep were really thin!). Thomas Harrison, one of whose family were later to endow Merchant Taylor's school, talked to the merchants who were scouring the farms looking for reliable supplies of quality wool to sell in the cities of Flanders. They told tales of the fortunes being made by the mill owners of Antwerp. Slowly the people began to realise that there was a world out there and money to be made. As the generations passed, the value of education, at least basic numeracy and literacy, was seen. The improvement in the quality of housing saw much better conditions for the people of Great Crosby, although still huddled around the well, the chapel and the green. One could be forgiven for assuming that there was no provision for the sick and the widow – always a sign of a civilised society. Widowhood could mean total destitution. The wealthier tenants of the town, (the term is relative), got together and formed the Great Crosby Benevolent Society in 1798. It was established *'for the purpose of Relieving the Members thereof in Old Age, Sickness and Infirmity'*. Meetings were held in Crosby Chapel, or occasionally in the Ship Inn. Membership was restricted to men between the ages of eighteen and thirty living within a mile of the chapel. Soldiers, sailors and miners were excluded. Any one found to be over thirty when joining was immediately expelled. As with many insurance based schemes only low risk members were accepted. The age thirty rule was sensible when one considers that the life expectancy of a Lancashire male in 1800 was about 35 – lower than any modern African nation. The joining fee was three shillings and sixpence, plus four pence for the book of rules, and the annual subscription was twelve shillings. If a member became sick and could not work he was given seven shillings a week for one year, then three shillings a week thereafter. On death five pounds was given to the estate, provided that he had been a member for at least twelve months and was not in arrears. The annual meeting -attendance compulsory- took place on the first Tuesday in January in the chapel. This was the business meeting followed by a sermon from the incumbent, and entertainment at a cost of one shilling. The rule book contained a long list of fines

for various misdemeanours. These included drunkenness, cursing, interrupting the chairman, seditious comments and the wearing of a hat (only the chairman had that privilege). The fines ranged from two pence to five shillings. Presumably wearing a hat came under 'disagreeably dressed' – fine two pence. On the death of a member attendance at the funeral, properly dressed, was mandatory but three pence worth of ale was allowed to be consumed.

The women began to sell the excess produce from their houses – gradually the idea of the farm shop was born. We seem to have come full circle on this. Then of course there was the ale-house. By the 1700s hops were being imported from Europe and ale became beer.

The monasteries were great brewers and always provided beer or ale to any passing travellers. It is reported that in some of these the monks were rationed to two gallons of beer a day. One has to assume that hard-working farmers would be thirstier than this! Bear in mind the beer was a lot weaker than it is today.

The first national tax was imposed on brewing in 1188 to pay for the Crusades – 'Saladin's Tax'. It was widely ignored. The ale-tasters or ale conners travelled about the country looking for evaders and also checking the quality of the brew. They wore leather trousers and would arrive at an establishment, pour a pool of ale on a wooden bench and then sit in it. Good adhesion indicated a high level of unfermented sugar and therefore a higher tax. This was somewhat unfair as the

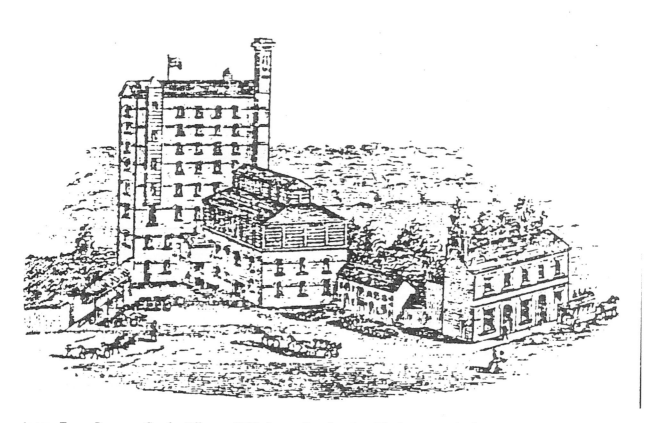

ABOVE Tower Brewery, Crosby Village c.1890, from a line drawing. The houses at the front are Gerrard Gardens.

level of unfermented sugar was a personal taste rather than one of quality.

In 1393 Richard II passed act making it compulsory for ale-houses to exhibit signs to identify them to the ale-tasters. They were also helpful to show the illiterate where pub was, and were useful advertising

Since 1495 the local magistrate or reeve could close an ale-house, which acquired a reputation for rowdy behaviour, and since 1552 it has been necessary to apply for an annual licence. Inns had been established as a monastic duty since the twelfth century but the village or urban pub as we know it only appeared in the late 1600s with Henry VIII's dissolution of the monasteries. As ale and beer was sold from the cottages of the lady brewers (brewsters), it is impossible to place

or date the first pub in Crosby Village. Nicholas Blundell's diary mentions several but some of these may not have been in Great Crosby. A favourite of his was Anne Rothwell's, which was almost certainly a cottage at the junction of Dibbs Lane, Delph Lane, Back Lane and Little Crosby Road. Anne Rothwell herself died in 1727. There was an inn on the site of the 'George' since the late 1700s. England had four King Georges between 1714 and 1830. It was probably opened to take advantage of the increased trade from the Goose Feast. Crosby village even had its own brewery. There had been one on the site of the present Sainsbury's car park for many years and had its outlet in a pub called variously the Crosby Vaults or the Brewery Vaults. Thomas

Molyneux demolished the brewery, but kept the pub, and, in 1884 built the state of the art Tower Brewery on the site. This was eight stories and one hundred feet high and must have been a very dominant landmark. Molyneux advertised 9 gallons of best ale at ten shillings (50p) distributed free to private families. The eight stories were necessary for current brewing practice, and used the height and gravity for the process. It measured fifty feet by twenty and normally produced 500 thirty-six gallon barrels a day. This output could be doubled if necessary. Many visitors came to see the brewery, including some from rival companies, and were impressed with its operation. Apart from supplying the Crosby Vaults, adjacent to the brewery, almost on the Green, and about where Sainsbury's off-licence now stands, Molyneux supplied the Hightown Hotel and several pubs in Liverpool. The brewery had long gone by the time that the Crosby Vaults was closed in 1929.

The Ship Inn was opened in the 1850s and finally closed its doors in 1925. Around 1865 it was briefly known as the Greyhound Hotel. The Old Church House Inn dates from about the same period and stood opposite the St. Michael's chapel on the site now occupied by the Sandalwood retirement flats.

Crosby's Goose Feast began as the ceremony of dressing the cross with flowers on St. Michael's Day, October 16th. On the first Sunday after this date two of the village inns, the George and the Ship offered a goose dinner.

Over the following four days a fair was held with the usual attractions as well as trying to climb the greasy pole and trying to catch a well-soaped pig. A market was held on the green with rows of stalls selling locally produced hot and cold food as well as ribbons and buttons etc. brought in from the big fairs at Preston or Chester. These were popular and very crowded. So next time you are pushing your trolley around Sainsbury's on a Saturday afternoon remember that you are doing what people were doing 250 years ago on exactly the same spot! There was however a down side to the Goose Feast. With the improvement in transport links to Liverpool many people of the 'rough and rowdy' type descended on the fair. What we would no longer consider acceptable was practised, dog-fighting, bull-baiting and cock-fighting and bare knuckle fighting. Fuelled by alcohol and perceived cheating (all of these events attracted a considerable level of gambling), the authorities found it hard to control, especially in the immediate vicinity of the two pubs. With the tighter regulations concerning the award and renewal of licences for the local inns, the Goose Feast eventually simply withered away although one could still take part as late as 1870.

During the late nineteenth century, and continuing today Great Crosby moved steadily from an agricultural community to a residential area complete with all the necessary service facilities. Although there has been very little manufacturing industry, Great Crosby has been near the cutting edge

ABOVE Old George Hotel and Myerscough's garage, Crosby Village.

of technology in some fields, brick making, brewing and state of the art protective clothing for industry and the military. There is the possibility of some small industries as shown in some of the road names. Just off the village was Kilnyard Lane, which implies an involvement with pottery. At the end of this lane was a group of houses called Sawyer's Cottages. A sawyer was a worker with wood but of course they could have been named after a Mr. Sawyer.

The marl pits scattered all over the district were mainly used for producing fertiliser, whereupon the resultant excavations were filled with water for fish farming, or simply allowed to fill with rain and abandoned. Many of these were later rather poorly filled in before houses were built upon the site. This may be the reason for the land subsidence that affects much of the town. At least one of the larger pits, on the site of the present Valewood School, was used as a source of clay for the manufacture of bricks.

By the 1870s Crosby Village was beginning to acquire the trappings of a vibrant centre of community life. Most of the property was still cottages but several more substantial houses were being built. The Georgian 'Old House' on Little Crosby Road had was already fifty years old, further north the larger house called 'Brookfield' was nearly as old. The Old House became empty in the 1960s and was vandalised beyond repair. It was demolished in 1973 to make way for the new houses opposite Richmond Road. Brookfield was demolished after 1918. Another imposing

ABOVE *The original site of the cross in Crosby Village. The gap between the buildings on the left is Clifton Avenue.*

residence was Stanley House on the corner of Moor Lane and Liverpool Road. This was built about the same time as the Old House and was pulled down in the 1880s. Sherburn Villa stood on the present site of the junction of Richmond Road and Little Crosby Road. It was demolished in 1938. Shops specializing in various commodities were appearing, butchers, fishmongers and those selling clothes and repairing shoes. There had been a police station on the village green since the 1840s. A permanent station, built on the site of the original stocks, pillory and ducking stool, dates from 1893. There were the beginnings of a voluntary fire service, several cafes and pubs, but no banks. Many transactions were based on barter, cash or traders tokens. Several of the local shops issued these traders tokens and a Crosby example is in the Warrington museum.

1880 saw the building of shops with accommodation above along both sides of Liverpool Road between the Green and Moor Lane, and a few at the village ends of Moor Lane and Cooks Road.

The first bank in the village was a branch of Parr's, near the Ship Inn. This was founded in 1890 and, in 1903, moved to the corner of Church Road, a site now occupied by Miss Tina's dress shop. It became the District Bank in 1923 and closed in 1966. The next was in the newly built mock-Tudor edifice on the corner of Moor Lane and Liverpool Road. The Bank of Liverpool had been founded in 1831 and opened its Crosby branch here in

1901. It became the Bank of Liverpool and Martins Bank in 1918, then Martins Bank in 1928 until the takeover by Barclays in 1969. It ceased to be a bank in 1984 when Barclays moved to their current premises.

A branch of Lloyds Bank opened on the site of the old Weirs garage building in 1962 and closed in 1983. This is now a charity shop run for Age Concern.

The London County and Westminster Bank opened a branch adjacent to the police station in 1918. This became the Westminster Bank in 1923 and the Nat West in 1968. The Midland Bank was based at 23 Liverpool Road until the move to Coronation Road in 1962

At No.20 Liverpool Road the Crosby Comrades Club replaced St. Peter and Pauls YMCA then moved to Crown Buildings in late 1950s and to its present site in Liverpool Road in 1972. An old passageway between Liverpool Road, and Islington, was once called The Weint.

If you asked shoppers in the village even now for directions to Clifton Avenue it would be interesting to know how many could help. It is a narrow entry between 9 and 11 Liverpool Road and until 1937 was called Moor Place, previously Moor Cottages, and served as the access to a row of terraced houses. The exit passageway was called Allengate. The property at 9 Liverpool Road was a pawnbrokers shop and had been owned by a Mrs. Amelia Benning since the 1890s. Although the address was officially Liverpool

Road Mrs. Benning had all her pledge cards and other stationery printed as Moor Place. This was to direct her clients to the side door in the narrow passageway to provide them with the necessary discretion. Traces of the door are still there. 1937 was a Coronation year and many residents wished to decorate their street and many requested a name change to something more in keeping with the occasion. A relevant change was ruled out as the words 'coronation', 'jubilee', 'royal' etc were already in use. The name Clifton Avenue was suggested and put to the residents of Moor Place. There was unanimous acceptance apart from the dissenting voice of Mrs. Benning. She not only refused to have anything to do with decorations, (or contributing to their cost), but refused to accept a change of address. At a meeting of the local council Mrs. Benning stated that for over forty years her business had always been known as the pawnbroker in Moor Place. She also objected that decorations would lower the tone of her establishment, and while they were discussing these matters could the council stop 'rough characters' and children riding bicycles down the narrow entry. There was also the matter of five years supply of printed stationery for which she demanded that the council compensate her should the name change go ahead. When asked whether there could be some compromise at this joyous time of celebration she retorted that she had no connection with the residents of Moor Place as she refused to deal with 'such people'. Obviously her preferred clients were from the more moneyed classes. All her objections were turned down, the only compromise that was reached was to change the name plate to 'Clifton Avenue, formally Moor Place' for a period of twelve months. As the passageway and the discreet side door remained unchanged, it is hard to believe that those clients with pledge tickets would not be able to find it. Moor Place along with Gerrard's Gardens and Richmond Terrace was demolished just before the Second World War. These last two rows of houses were previously called Gerrard's Cottages and Richmond Cottages and where built in the 1860s on what is now the north side of Sainsbury's car park and part of Richmond Road.

Most of the shops in the village sold food. There was also the Crosby Cocoa Rooms later the Dining Rooms and Supper Bar. Among these shops was the family business, Crowe's. This establishment was founded in the 1880s and was one of the first licensed grocers on Merseyside. Grocers could be licensed to sell spirits, liquors and sweets, NOT to be consumed on the premises. We may not know of the first pub, but Crowe's was almost certainly the first off-licence. It was often known as the Olde World Shop, and featured a hand carved solid mahogany counter and heavy brass scales. These were still in use when the shop finally closed in 1979, just short of its centenary.

As part of the development to incorporate the new Sainsbury's supermarket and improve congestion in Crosby Village all the shops between De Villiers Avenue and Liverpool Road were demolished by 1982. These included several long standing establishments such as Abberleys store; Duffy's the chimney sweep and the local office of the National Coal Board. Earlier versions of these shops and houses were called Rookery Cottages. Gerrard Gardens and Richmond Terrace had been cleared in 1939 and the way was now clear to build Richmond Road to link Little Crosby Road and Moor Lane. This also eventually facilitated the construction of the supermarket car park in the 1980s. Liver Terrace built in the 1850s, was demolished in 1966.

The Crosby Herald office is now in the centre of Crosby. As the Waterloo and Crosby Herald till 1937 it had its offices in South Road moved to Church Road, Waterloo in1939 and Village 1992.

With the increase of motor traffic between Liverpool and Southport a by-pass was planned to take this traffic away from the congested village centre. Although the plan was first mooted in the 1930s, twenty years and the Second World War intervened. The work started in 1957 with the demolition of the row of shops opposite Islington down to the Methodist chapel. Amongst these was a small court of houses originally called Henry's Place, changed to Langan's Place in 1874. One side of the new road was opened in January 1958 and the official opening took

ABOVE Islington. These shops, including the Chinese laundry, were demolished in 1936.

place in June. The section of Liverpool Road between the 'George' and Sainsbury's was pedestrianised in 1993 and the rest of the village followed with the closing of the Moor Lane area to traffic in 1995. With the demolition of most of the original shops in the 1970s and 1980s and the advent of Sainsbury's supermarket many of the food outlets have gone to be replaced by a plethora of wine bars and estate agents. The need for car parking space has seen the demise of many old buildings. Looking at the car park to the east of Liverpool Road it is hard to believe it once contained Moor Place, Sherburn Villa, Richmond Terrace, Gerard Gardens, and the Tower Brewery. The park to the west once boasted the original chapel, the boy's school, the village green (with at least two inns) and the local police station.

In the early part of the twentieth century no town, even one as small as Great Crosby, was without its Chinese laundry. Mr Yee You opened his in Islington in about 1912. In those days Islington ran from the corner of Church Road round to Liverpool Road. The section that runs from Livock and Edward's garage to Liverpool Road is now part of Coronation Road. The Chinese laundry, along with the other shops in the block, was pulled down in 1936. The laundry was almost certainly on the site what is now called the Hong Kong and Shanghai Bank! The laundry found a new home in Victoria Road.

COOKS ROAD

The road that straggled northwards from Crosby Village to the outlying farms has been known as Cooks Road or Cooks Lane since at

RIGHT Grapes Hotel and tram terminus, Victoria Road/ Cooks Road.

ABOVE Line drawing of Pinfold Cottage, Cooks Road.

least the late 1700s. It was often known as Old Lane but this appears to be a local usage, as that name does not appear on any old maps. If there ever was a Mr. Cook, or more likely Farmer Cook he has disappeared from the record. The section of the road between Little Crosby Road and the Halsall Girl's School was known as Pinfold Lane until about 1880. The Pinfold was on the Village green next to the police station with the pinder's cottage nearby. Beyond the Halsall School was one of Crosby's many lost pubs. The Grapes Hotel was opposite the junction of Victoria Road and was built in the 1840s. It was demolished in about 1912 to make way for road widening. Although always known as the Grapes it was listed by the local licensing authorities from 1900 as the 'Boar's Head'. The reported weekly takings in 1905 were £26, the average profit was £5, and fixtures and fittings were valued at £15. This pub was one of the many in Crosby supplied with beer from Thorougood's Brewery, based in Queen Street in Waterloo. To the rear of the Grapes was a row of houses called Lathom, later Lupton's Cottages, demolished in 1970. The Lupton family was one of Great Crosby's biggest farmers.

On the other side of Cooks Road there were a number of other thatched cottages as well as the Pinfold cottage. Alexandra Road was named after the Princess of Wales, a renowned beauty and leader of fashion. Most of the road was built in the late 1880s.

LEFT Cooks Road. The original Birkey Hotel is on the right.

Princess Alexandra had to wait until her husband became king in 1901 before Crosby named a hall and a park after her. On the opposite corner, the present site of Pinfold Court was Massam's the grocers, which eventually became a Liverpool Co-operative Society store. Just behind was the Orchard Farm and Dairy. This was replaced by the Express Dairy and is now the flats called Pinfold Court. One of the thatched cottages was bought in 1955 with the idea of turning it into a pottery complete with facilities for teaching the art, and a shop. During the renovations a small shoe filled with lavender was found in the roof beams. Experts dated it to the mid 1500s. How it got there and how it had never been found before remains a mystery, could it have been a sixteenth century air freshener? Its discovery adds to the terrible loss to the village of several Elizabethan buildings as recently as 1963. Further along towards Victoria Road was Lottie Squires' tea shop, known as the

Cockatoo Café. The bird was kept in a cage outside the premises (or in the entrance if wet) and was a good talker much to the entertainment of the patrons. Next door was the Birkey Hotel. The original building was built in the 1840s and was pulled down and replaced with the present structure about 1920. The derivation of the word 'Birkey' is a mystery. The current sign shows a group of gentlemen discussing weighty matters around a tree stump. A 'birk' in old Lancashire dialect was a birch tree (from the Icelandic 'bjork') A fourteenth century Scottish poem has the line '*than byrkis on athyr sid the way*'. This seems to signify regular meetings at the birch tree each year in the month of athyr, (November).

Most of Cambridge Avenue was built in the 1870s as was the row of three storey houses to the north of the junction. Beyond that was farming country which pastured cows for the Big Pit Farm in Victoria Road and those for the many dairies in the town. One large building dominated the left side of Cooks Lane – the Crosby brickworks. It was not the first; that was in Forefield Lane, but was apparently the most successful. The Cooks Lane works was built on one of Crosby's largest marl pits, and dates from the mid 1890s. In 1898 the owner of the Great Crosby Brick Company in Cooks Lane, (on the site of what is now Valewood School), Mr Edward Peters introduced mechanical brick making machinery. Although his 40 workers had to actually dig the clay from twenty feet depth in the adjacent marl-pit, his new machinery could produce 25-30 thousand bricks a day. This was ten times the manual method. As an illustration it took one day to produce enough bricks for a small cottage and five days for a grand detached house. In 1899 Peters secured the contract to supply the bricks for the new St. Faith's church. The 700,000 bricks needed could be supplied within a month. It was Mr. Peters' workers who found and removed the glacial boulder which now stands in Coronation Park. The factory finally ran out of clay and closed in 1920. An article in the Crosby Herald of 1921 extols the virtues of Crosby – the sea air and the near countryside, but wished that the Blundells would open up Crosby Woods (done in 1935) and that the derelict brick works would be cleared up.

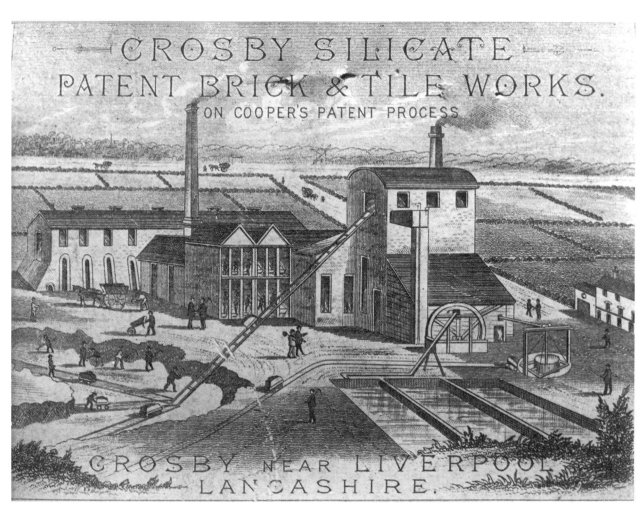

ABOVE Great Crosby Brick Company.

Edward Peters was very involved in local | politics. In 1896 at age of 30 he was elected councillor for the St. Johns Ward, the youngest member of the Crosby council.

In 1912 Cooks Lane, which now started from Victoria Road, was renamed Manor Road with great plans for the extension of the Crosby housing stock over the fields to right and left. At this time the only building to the north of the brick works was White Cottage owned by the local farming family the Somervilles. It is often called Somerville Cottage. In 1866 Henry Usher and his family moved their rope making business from Liverpool to Crosby. They settled at No. 13 Alma Vale and established the business in Cooks Lane roughly between where Manor Drive and St. Michaels Road now run. It consisted of a long barn type structure where the long lengths of twine could be stretched and plaited to form the necessary thickness of rope. This type of building was known as a rope walk. In 1871 Henry moved over Liverpool Road to York Road and in the early 1880s he was joined by Levi, who moved into No. 3 Lune Street, and Thomas who lived at No. 13 Hornby Street. Henry left the firm in 1890 and it was then run as Levi and Thomas Usher from an office at No 89 Victoria Road until 1894 when it was taken over by the rope makers Radcliffe and Brown. This became S.J.Radcliffe and Company in 1898 and had one of the earliest telephone numbers, Waterloo 231. By 1904 the rope walk was no more. Further on was White Stones Lane.

This was approximately on the site of St. Michaels Road and led to a geological out-crop called the 'white stones', about where the junction of Cambridge Road now is. These may have been used to mark the boundary between the good agricultural land and the salt marsh.

The First World War halted the housing plans but by 1927 building was well under way. Ince Avenue was one of the first. At that time it stretched from Cambridge Road across Manor Road to Little Crosby Road. The latter section soon had a name change to Ilford Avenue. By the end of the 1930s Manor Road was com-pletely developed, as was the area towards Little Crosby Road and westwards to Cambridge Road. The unmade track north-wards from the junction of St. Michaels Road to Hall Road was still called Cooks Lane until the proposed bungalow development in 1960. The new residents wished to continue to call it Cooks Lane in order to, in their words, preserve one of Crosby's ancient road names. However they were overruled and it became merely a continuation of Manor Road. By the time the Girls Secondary School was opened the length of St. Michaels Road, Manor Road and most of Hall Road were developed for housing. From the corner of Hall Road and Manor Road to Little Crosby, the track called Dibb Lane (from dibb meaning a small pond) gave access to Sniggery Woods, a gift from the Blundell family to the people of Crosby made for the jubilee of 1935. The pools and ditches are still there but the eels (the snigs) have gone.

RIGHT Moor Lane in the 1960s. Liver Terrace is on the right.

MOOR LANE

Moor Lane is featured on local maps as early as the 1700s as were some of the roads off it serving the scattered farms on the moor. Forefield Lane, Brown's Lane (now Chesterfield Road) and Gin Lane (now Chestnut Avenue) were muddy tracks until the start of extensive house building in the 1930s.

In the early 1880s Crosby Village was spreading along the first part of Moor Lane. Beyond the 'George' was a small row of houses called Moor Villas. Harrington's the funeral directors set up business between the George and Moor Villas in 1905. The Villas were demolished in the mid 1930s and Weirs garage occupied the site, which later became a bank and then a charity shop. The block of three storey shops called Moor Terrace featured two of Crosby's better known names. Miss Maude Smith set up her stationery business there in 1937 and her name is still over the same shop. A little further along the row there had always been a chemist's shop. This was the establishment of J.Allen Jones

between 1924 and 1936. Opposite Moor Terrace a few shops had replaced Stanley House. They included Callis's metal work shop and Poston's Tea and Coffee Rooms. These went when the mock Tudor bank building was built in 1901. From 1936 the Moor Lane shopping area steadily expanded. Tesco came and went in the 1970s. Bobby's tobacconists was established in the early 1950s and replaced by the Kwiksave supermarket in 1974. Richmond Road finally achieved an outlet to Moor Lane with the demolition of Liver Terrace and the construction of the flats 'Avon Court', in 1966.

Of the cottages near the junction with Scape Lane (once called Scab Lane), and those near what is now Moor Drive, many still remain. Most of the larger houses have gone. Those called The Grove, opposite Richmond Road have been converted into flats but their essential character remains. Moor House was demolished in 1961 to make way for the modern block of flats that bear its name. The more modern housing extends up to the boundary between Great Crosby and Thornton and beyond. One of the original triangular boundary stones once marked this but it has now disappeared. The area to the north of Moor Lane features three well known Crosby sites; the Tithebarn, the Northern Club amongst the fine houses of Moor Park, and the Crosby Windmill.

The Tithebarn had some connection with the parish of Sefton but its origins are unknown. The original building was reputedly converted into a coaching inn in about 1825 but this is doubtful, as Moor Lane was not on any of the normal coaching routes. If true it would have gone the way of most of the coaching inns with the coming of the railway in the 1850s. The site became a small group of houses called Tithebarn Cottages in 1890. One of these was a laundry and was apparently set up to take women off the streets and give them gainful employment. The large sheets were set out to dry on the acres of gorse bushes in the area – must have been an amazing sight. The cottages were purchased by some of the local Masonic lodges in 1955 and opened as a home for Masonic dependents on October 17th 1956. The part of the original Tithebarn still remaining was old enough to have its fair share of stories of hauntings and even buried treasure. The men from Costain's, who were working on the conversion and extension, often complained of unexplained footsteps.

The first mill in the area was on the Blundell estate at Little Crosby. The first date is unknown but it was operating in 1275.

A later one was built on the site now occupied by St. Peter and Paul's church, Liverpool Road. This was operating by 1290 and was destroyed in a storm of 1565. Another mill was recorded at the time but its whereabouts are unknown.

As the control over corn milling slipped away from the lord of the manor it was decided that a mill nearer the centre of Crosby Village, and on higher ground to take advantage of the prevailing wind, was more relevant to the population's needs. The Little Crosby Mill was demolished in May 1813. The site chosen was at the highest point within the Great Crosby boundary, and much of the mechanical parts from Little Crosby were used in its construction. It was built by the engineer William Murray of Durham at a cost of £691 1s 10d., and was completed by early 1814. A miller's house was built in 1821. A great storm of January 1839 set the sails spinning so fast that there was a danger of fire to the mill from the overheated gear wheels. Naturally a windmill could only operate when there was wind, which wasn't necessarily that convenient. By 1855 an auxiliary steam engine was installed and in 1892 the mill became solely steam powered. By 1900 the sails, the balcony and the fantail, the device that kept the sails pointing into the wind, had gone. Electricity replaced steam in the 1940s. There was a plan to demolish the mill and develop the site for housing in the 1970s.

This caused uproar and was quietly dropped. Since 1972 it has ceased to be a working mill.

The roads off Moor Lane to the south are largely the domain of post 1930 housing although the roads themselves are of great antiquity. Forefield Lane boasted one of the largest marl pits in Crosby and was the base for the Crosby Brick and Terra Cotta Works. This is now the site of Forefield Lane Primary School. (Crosby Council seemed to have had a penchant for building primary schools over large marl pits – as Valewood School in Manor Road). Along what is now Elmwood Avenue a track called Fishers Lane led to Moorside Farm. Its continuation, Moorside Road, was once called Piggy Lane. This is far more likely to be local use and is never officially recorded as such. To the south of Moor Lane, and parallel to it runs Brownmoor Lane, probably named for the colour of the bracken. This was the usual collection of small cottages and farms. One of the larger farms was called Isle of Man. Presumably the original owner had some connection with the island. As often happens in this situation an area of several surrounding dwellings took the name Isle of Man, which may well have caused some confusion to map makers of the time. There was another Isle of Man Cottage on Marsh Lane (College Road).

The Northern Club was founded as the Northern Cricket Club in Rawson Road, Seaforth in 1859. In 1878 the land was sold for housing and the club moved to Haig Road, Waterloo Park. The present land was purchased in 1907. The sports facilities were used by the military in both world wars. During 1939 to 1945 period members were allowed to use the sports ground at the Hightown Club.

Leonard Myerscough one of Crosby's pioneering motorists lived at 52 Moor Lane. He set up a bicycle shop in Seaforth in 1898 and founded a family that owned, sold and even raced and rallied cars and motorcycles for the next 75 years.

LIVERPOOL ROAD

Liverpool Road has existed in name since the late 1700s, and maybe for many years before that. The first section, now pedestrianised, from the village green to the junction with Islington and Moor Lane is described under 'Village'. Its length, from Moor Lane to College Road, of about three quarters of a mile, has included three churches, five schools, and two preparatory schools, two or maybe three hotels, two cinemas, many large houses and many modest ones, including some of the oldest in the district. The row of houses to the north of St. Peter and Pauls Church are dated 1826. It is now part of the A 565, the main artery between Liverpool and Southport and can become very congested at times. Plans for a relief road direct from the motorway links to Southport have been on the table for many years. This would at least stop much of the congestion. Patience may be rewarded – Crosby had to wait twenty years for the by pass to ease the congestion in the village.

ABOVE The Crosby cannon.

The Crosby Hotel was built in the 1830s and was a Total Abstinence hotel until about 1870, when the York Road and Queens Road area was being developed. An interesting feature of the hotel is the Crosby cannon. Many pubs, including the Crosby, had a public weighbridge on the frontage. This was for farmers to weigh their produce on the way to market so that they could have some idea as to its value. Presumably at some time the farmer would have taken his empty cart to the weighbridge to ascertain its unladen weight. After the building of St. Luke's church, in 1854, the heavy cart wheels were repeatedly

damaging the sandstone wall of the church-yard. To protect the wall the barrel of a large iron cannon was cemented into the corner. Placed at an angle it was designed to keep the wheels away from the church wall. It was so successful that it remains there to this day long after the weighbridge and the farm carts have gone. Its origin however is a mystery.

The Islington Hotel was built in the 1850s on the corner of Vale Road. It was a victim of the 1935 road widening scheme that included all the properties from Vale Road round to Livock and Edwards's garage. The licence was taken over by the newly built Copplehouse in Fazakerley. It was badly missed as one of Crosby's busiest pubs taking over £5,000 a year. The brewery, Threlfall's, demanded a large compensation payment from Crosby Council.

Vale Road contains some of Crosby's older houses, built in the late 1850s. It was original-ly named Alma Vale after the Crimean War battle. The name was changed to Vale Road about 1914. The row of terraced cottages in Alma Vale was named Cyprus Terrace.

St Luke's Road was originally called Lorimer's Lane. A lorimer was a maker of spurs and other small metal parts used by horsemen. The name was changed to Bond's Lane in about 1870. This name may have had some connection with the family of Ralph Bond's, founder of the Crosby Cow Club. Its current name dates from 1906.

Crosby's first cinema, the 'Crosby Picture House' was opened on 6th December 1913.

Its initial success was probably due to its obtaining sole area rights to screen every new Charlie Chaplin film. The cinema closed in 1916 and was taken over for use as St. Luke's parish hall until 1972 when it became the new home of the Crosby Comrades Club.

After the demise of the Picture House and the end of the First World War there was a resurgence of enthusiasm for the cinema. The Corona in College Road had opened in 1920 and another was built and opened next door to the ex- Picture House. The Regent Cinema and Café was opened on 11th December 1920. Very unusually the café was run from above the cinema foyer. Sound films came in 1930 and the café continued to be very popular until its closure in 1946. The cinema itself closed in 1968 and became a Mecca bingo hall. Since 1994 it has been St. Mary's Sports Centre. A tree opposite to the cinemas is obviously not a film fan. Ever since it's planting in about 1910 it has had a persistent leaning away from them!

Of the many large houses in Liverpool Road two are worth a mention. The Mulberries was the home of the Bousefield family and has a garden sundial dated 1765. It became an integral part of Merchant Taylors Girls School in 1911.

Crosby House was bought in 1897 from the Myers family by the Poor Sisters of Nazareth as an orphanage, for £5,000. It was eventually renamed Nazareth House.

The Myers family had been successful landowners, brokers and bankers in the Preston area for generations. It became apparent, in the late 1700s, that there was considerable money to be made in Liverpool. John Myers bought a large piece of land which included several small holdings as well as the original Crosby House in 1779. In that year he was married in Sefton church. He died in 1820 but the family's finances went from strength to strength. They were important in the endowment of many churches and schools in the area and in about 1840 the road that runs off Liverpool Road next to Crosby House was called Myers Lane, later Myers Road and then Myers Road East. After the sale of the house what was left of the family moved to Oxfordshire.

ENDBUTT LANE

There are some doubts as to the derivation of the name of this road. Often quoted is one that it comes from End-boat Lane, the route from Crosby centre to the boat stop on the Leeds and Liverpool Canal. However, this is not named as such on any maps nor in any census returns, although it may have been in use during the canal craze of the 1820s. It does have a former name – Henbutt Lane attributed to the fact that it was a centre for small holdings specialising in poultry. It is marked as this on many old maps and on the first census returns up to1861

Enfield House was built in the late 1850s and was famous as the birthplace of J. Bruce Ismay, chief executive of the White Star Line, and a survivor of the 'Titanic'. The house was demolished in the 1920s to make way for Enfield Avenue.

In the early 1900s Kershaw Binns and Company were already established with London and Manchester offices. A factory was built for the manufacture of cotton bags on the present site of Kershaw Avenue in 1911. The factory diversified into the production of linen, calico and stockinette, mutton and beef covering cloth and a proprietary cleaning cloth called 'Kit'. For most of the period 1914 to 1918 Kershaw's were involved in the making of bandages for the war effort. They became a limited company in 1920 with headquarters in Manchester and the factory telephone number was Crosby 133. The works closed in 1938.

Littlewoods Mail Order Company was established in Old Hall Street in Liverpool in 1932. Post war expansion forced them to look for larger premises to deal with orders. The company moved to the vacant site in Kershaw Avenue in 1951, and is now one of the town's largest employers.

Mary Lunt and her husband Peter founded the Victoria Soap Works in 1886 on the site now occupied by Brookside Court. At that time Endbutt Lane was a very rural location so presumably there was very little problem with pollution. Peter became more involved in the business in 1888 and took over the firm in 1891. The business moved to Collingwood Street in Liverpool in 1894 and the Endbutt Lane works was demolished soon after.

Blaco built a small factory in Musker Street making electrical conduit fittings in January 1934. This led to a development of small factories replacing the row of houses named Musker's Cottages.

Moorgate Street was developed in the 1870s and changed its name to Moorgate Avenue in 1924. An entry by No.12 leads to a grassy track once a row of terraced cottages called Hill Street.

The story of the original Endbutt Hotel is also that of the Independent Methodist chapel now in Seafield Avenue, see page 33.

COLLEGE ROAD

Since the late 1700s a track from the south end of the Liverpool road skirted the Crosby marsh to join with the pathway leading from Crosby village to the sea. Not surprisingly this was later to be called Marsh Lane. Its extension northwards to some outlying farms became known as Old Marsh Lane, now College Road North. To complement the change of Out Lane to Victoria Road, Marsh Lane became Albert Road in 1871.

By 1880 the only houses in the area were the large properties between the corner plot later to house Merchant Taylors Boys School, and Myers Road West, and other larger houses in Myers Road itself. With the plans to build the imposing Merchant Taylors School in 1879 a petition of these residents demanded a change of name, so, in 1882, with the official completion of the school, the road became College Road. By 1890 some of the

ABOVE College Road, c.1905, looking towards Congregational church.

roads off College Road were being built and Victoria Park was being laid out. Some isolated streets off the road, Brookfield Avenue, Brighton Road and Rossett Road were built and the first shops began to open. Much of this area was designed and built by local builder Mr. Rossett Rogers, hence the name Rossett Road and the sports ground, Rossett Park.

The Edinburgh Arms was established in 1895 on the corner of Brighton Road and changed its name to the Edinburgh Inn about 1910. Brighton Road was a long row of smaller terraced houses down to the railway. It included a mission hall run from St. Nicholas church on the right and a few shops. There is anecdotal but no official record of an establishment at the railway end of Brighton Road called the Swan Hotel. If it existed at all it was probably only selling beer from a front room. The mission would have been very unhappy to be in the centre of a road with a pub at each end and would have tried to close the unofficial one. Brighton Road became Jubilee Road to celebrate King George V's twenty-five years on the throne, in 1935. The fields to the south of Brighton Road, where Sunnyside Road now runs, became a military camp between 1914 and 1918. Also on this site, fronting College Road, Frodsham's Garage was established, in the early 1920s. In spite of many changes of ownership there has been a motor repair business or at least a petrol filling station on this site ever since.

Cows from the dairy in Myers Road, near the corner of College Road, grazed on the fields between Myers Road and Brookfield Avenue. There was a dairy there until the 1970s but the cows had to go elsewhere when the Lancaster Avenue/Kingswood Drive estate was built in the 1930s. This estate was planned as early as 1905 but the building of larger houses in Coronation Drive and Woodville Avenue necessitated some modifications to the original plan. Kingswood Drive was originally to be called Queens Drive and Brunswick Road, and Marlborough Road, Tudor Road. Tudor Road was originally Plantaganet Road and. Lancaster Avenue was Gloucester Avenue. The original site for Lancaster Avenue, between Woodville and Warwick Avenues, was eliminated to allow for their larger gardens. Earl's Close and The Spur were eventually built on this site.

The junction of College Road and Coronation Road had been an important part of the town for many years as the domain of Crosby's most important resident, the town bull. This was known as the Bullcroft. It was ideally placed as the civic centre for Great Crosby.

By the 1870s a venue for entertainments as well as a meeting place and offices for the Great Crosby Urban District Council was becoming a necessity. The council had been meeting in a house in Victoria Road, which was totally inadequate. A very impressive building to be called the Great Crosby Assembly Rooms was opened on 14th November 1888 by Lady Forwood, wife of Sir William Forwood of 'Ramleh' Burbo Bank Road and recently Lord Mayor of Liverpool. At this time Thorpes Lane followed the present line of Coronation Road up to just

RIGHT Alexandra Hall 1888–2002.

beyond Regent Road and then along what is now Carnegie Avenue. As well as accommodation for the Local Board Offices and council chamber, the Rooms featured a hall, supper room, and cloakroom, kitchen, and staff quarters. The centrepiece was a seven feet wide staircase leading to a large reception room and concert hall/ballroom. At the opening ceremony Lady Forwood was presented with a key pendant and a gold bracelet. This was followed by entertainment and dancing until 1 a.m. In 1902 the building was renamed Alexandra Hall in honour of the new queen. In 1954 it was the venue for the ceremony to induct the first freeman of the borough, Earl Alexander, the Minister of Defence. It has been an entertainment centre since. It was well used during the Merseybeat era of the early 1960s, on January 19th 1961 an up and coming group called the Beatles performed there. The local magistrate's court met in the Hall between 1977 and 1992. The building was steadily closed down as the Sefton council offices were moved to Bootle and Southport. It was finally demolished in 2002 to make way for a block of flats called Alexandra Court. To the architect's credit it has not only kept the name but also the superficial outline of the original Hall.

The local fire brigade had started as a largely voluntary organisation in the 1880s based on the village green. In 1894 it had achieved some official recognition and had a new headquarters to the rear of the Assembly Rooms, the present site of the Service Club. In 1960 it moved to Crosby Road North, Waterloo.

Close by was to be the town's first public library. Andrew Carnegie, the Scottish steel magnate who at one time was the richest man in the world, endowed nearly 3,000 libraries throughout the English speaking world. His first was in his home town of Dunfermline in 1883 and the one on College Road, opened in June1905, was a much later beneficiary.

Rossett Park is now well known as the home ground of Marine Football Club, one of Crosby's biggest sporting successes. Marine A.F.C was formed at a meeting of enthusiasts at the Marine Hotel in South Road, Waterloo in 1894. They had immediate success in the local leagues and have done regularly ever since. The move to Rossett Park in 1903 gave Marine a permanent home. The high point was probably the 1932 Amateur Cup Final played at the ground of the London team West Ham. Unfortunately they lost 1-7 to Dulwich Hamlet. One record they can be proud of is having the longest serving manager in any professional or amateur team in Roly Howard, one of Crosby's great characters.

'Lord' George Sangster's Circus purchased the land between Rossett Road and Mersey Road, called Marsh Field, in about 1880. Various travelling acts performed on the site, pierrots, Collins and Willis' Bobby Horses and performing bears. These bears, chained to the owner, went house-to-house rattling a tin cup for donations. (Shutting the door in the face not recommended!). One was a wrestling

ABOVE Line drawing of the Corona cinema, College Road.

bear who, so the barker said, had travelled the world and never been thrown until he met Jamie Rimmer of Jubilee (then Brighton) Road! Jamie apparently won the five-pound prize very easily. The circus departed in 1914 never to return. A more sedate entertainment in the form of the Corona cinema was built on the site. Plans for the cinema were considered as soon as the circus left town but the First World War intervened. It was eventually finished and opened in 1920, and, on 31st March 1930 became one of the first cinemas with sound in the Liverpool area. It closed on 1st December 1956 and was demolished in 1957. Shops, including Image and David's Cakes, now occupy the site.

CORONATION ROAD

A grassy track leading from part of Crosby Village out towards the sea was known as Thorp or Thorp's Lane since the early 1800s. Who Mr. Thorp was, is now lost, although Thorpe's dwelling and small holding was on the site of Halsall School in Cooks Road. On several maps of the 1840s it was called Harp's Lane, but this may have been a copying error, the 1841 census refers to it as Thorp Lane. Even in the mid-1880s there was very little building on this road, just a few humble cottages near the Islington junction. The road initially stopped at about Regent Road but by 1890 it wound its way along what is now Carnegie Avenue and across to Mersey Road.

73

Shaftesbury Road was built about 1890 followed by Florence Terrace in 1899 and Harrington Road in 1900. In 1900 the road was considerably improved and extended along the side of the Council headquarters in the Assembly Rooms in order to improve the area's civic pretensions, and to line up with Mersey Road as a direct line to the railway. To celebrate the coronation of Edward VII and Queen Alexandra, in 1902, Thorp Lane was changed to Coronation Road and the Assembly Rooms were changed to Alexandra Hall. The area around the Hall had been given as a gift to the people of Crosby. Mr George Rodway, a prominent Blundellsands solicitor, petitioned the local residents to utilise this land. The services of Mr Exton, who owned the garden centre called the Victoria Nursery in Thorp Lane, were used to plan and lay out what is now Alexandra Park. It was opened in 1902. What is now Carnegie Avenue was still called Thorpe's Lane until 1910 when it was re-named in honour of the man who had endowed the town's public library. The Victoria Nursery is still there but called Carnegie Café and Garden Centre and is very much smaller.

A Drill Hall was built in 1911 for 7th Battalion King's Liverpool Regiment and the Prince of Wales' Volunteers (South Lancashire Regiment), 10th Reserve Battalion. These units were formed in Crosby in October 1914. Although they were never posted to the battle front, as a reserve battalion many individuals served in France. One of these, Gabriel Coury, won Crosby's only V.C. in 1916. He survived the war, died in 1956, and is buried in St Peter and Paul's churchyard. The hall became Crosby Youth Centre in 1967.

The Blundell family made a gift of land on the south side of Thorps Lane, as a park, with bowling greens and flower beds, for the

LEFT Boulder stone on the village site before 1926.

pleasure of the people of Great Crosby. This was called the Recreation Ground and changed its name to Coronation Park in 1906. The boating lake was opened in June 1931. A distinguishing feature of the park is the large glacial boulder sited near the main entrance. It is believed that this brought down from the Lake District by an ice age glacier several thousands years ago. It was discovered by the workers at the Great Crosby Brick Company in Cooks Lane in 1898 and was presented to the council by the owner of the company, Edward Peters. Soon afterwards he was then elected on to the local council. It was carefully excavated from the marl pit and taken by a team of horses to its first site at the junction of Islington and Liverpool Road, and was surrounded by iron railings and placed in the direction of travel of its original journey. On 5th July 1921 it formed a background to a royal visit. The Prince of Wales, later Edward VIII, stopped off at the boulder whilst travelling from Southport to Liverpool. He met councillors and many ex-servicemen. In 1926 it was decided to move the boulder to Coronation Park. A steam traction engine was used and very slowly pulled the stone the short distance to its new home. It took three days to cover the quarter of a mile and place it on a pedestal in the park, still facing its original direction.

About 1900 Miriam Gertrude Mills decided to forego the delights of millinery and went for a career as a pastrycook. In 1910, whilst working in the Lake District, she met and married Walter Satterthwaite. They immediately set up a baking business in Southport with £50 joint savings. After a lot of trials they discovered suitable premises for a bakery in Coronation Road. Supplying the shop in Southport became difficult so the couple decided to restrict their operations to Crosby and Waterloo. By about 1937 they had shops in South Road, College Road, Moor Lane and Crosby Road North. They both died in the 1970s when well into their nineties, but the company lives on. If you ask any ex-pat from Crosby what he or she misses most don't be surprised if they say 'a Sattie's pie'!

For lovers of good food Duckels delicatessen was a great loss. Established in 1910 it never lost its reputation but closed in 1988.

Until 1870 Mersey Road was simply an empty track with nothing to relieve the monotony except Crosby station and its adjoining level crossing. The only building beyond the railway was 'Warrenhouse', (Mersey Road was called Warrenhouse Lane up to 1870). The 'tin church' of St. Barnabas, stood on the sandhills about where Agnes Road now runs. Within ten years the station had been moved and the bridge had replaced the crossing, St. Nicholas church had been built. Several houses in Mersey Road and Harlech Road as well as the shops in Bridge Road were under construction. The road then continued as Mariners Road to the coast guard station and the beach.

The Aintree Leather Company was founded on 1st April 1937 as leather merchants. They

RIGHT Bellions Court (Davies Place), now the Crows Nest car park, Victoria Road.

very soon found a niche market for the manufacture and supply of leather gloves for industrial use. They then opened a factory in Liverpool which became one of the many casualties of the May blitz of 1941. Relocation to Crosby was followed by the construction of a purpose built factory in Mersey Road, opened in 1950. As this was a family concern it was renamed Bennetts Gloves and, in 1979, Bennetts Safetywear Ltd. The company became a world leader in the use of glove knitting machines for the manufacture of heavy duty industrial gloves. Diversification has since followed and the company now makes a range of fashion gloves and other accessories as well as all forms of protective clothing for industry, police and the military, and exports all over the world.

A group of philanthropic 'ladies of Blundellsands' were operating a refuge for poor sick children of Liverpool based in a house in Wellington Street in Waterloo. They soon outgrew this and, in 1906 they bought a plot of land in Mariners Road for a Cottage Home. This is now the South Sefton Mencap Cottage.

VICTORIA ROAD

Victoria Road is one of Crosby's oldest roads. Listed as Out Lane from the early 1700s it is probably a lot older. Presumably the origin of the name was simply because it led out to the sea, but it may be from the provision of 'out-gates' to keep cattle from straying. Many of the properties that still line the road date from the mid 1800s, and were usually divided into small groups of cottages called terraces, or for the larger houses, villas. This system has been preserved in the building of Carlton Terrace in about 1905 and Claremont Terrace in the 1920s.

There were a few shops, an overflow from the village, at the Cooks Road end of

Victoria Road, but most of the properties were houses, some small but several very imposing villas. Most remain today. In 1891 David and Isabella Maitland opened their chandlers shop at No. 93. The shop is still there giving the same kind of service. Until about 1972 a row of shops occupied what is now Maitand's car park and garden centre. Amongst these were the Chinese laundry, which had moved from Islington in 1936, and the Fox Inn. This pub at 79 Victoria Road opened in the 1870s. It apparently had dubious reputation. In 1905 the police objected to renewal of the licence because of excessive drunkenness and its attraction of undesirables. The tenant William Blackburn had been blamed for his lack of control of the premises and fined twenty shillings and costs. His eighty five year old mother, the owner, was too old to take charge. The licence was renewed with a threat. It was due to be closed within a year, the owner being entitled to compensation. If in that time there was a recurrence of trouble the old lady would be put out without any compensation at all. One of the pleas made to renew the licence was that there were no other pubs within the immediate area. It depends what you mean by immediate. This writer, in the interests of research, stood at the site of the Fox's front door and measured the distance to the three nearest hostelries. The Crow's Nest was 26 paces away, The Birkey, 30 and the Grapes in Cooks Road, 38. The Fox Inn closed in1909 and became

St. Peter and. Paul's Young Men's Club which had moved from Liverpool Road in Crosby village. The premises spent some years as a shop; even a ladies' outfitters, and a private dwelling before its demolition in 1972.

The Crow's Nest was first opened in 1876. It has had its ups and downs but is now firmly placed in the traditional category, no games, no music, no machines, just good beer and good conversation. Long may it continue. Until the late 1950s the Crows' car park was the site of a group of small houses called variously Davies Place or Davies' Cottages, and later Bellion's Court.

Victoria Road ends at the junction with College Road but its predecessor, Out Lane, continued down to the sea. This stretch of road is now called Blundellsands Road. The road to the right, now College Road North was called Old Marsh Lane even as late as 1906. College Road was called Marsh Lane up to 1871.

The family firm of Robert Armstrong and sons started with furniture removals, horse drawn of course, at Rose Cottage, 39 Victoria Road in 1874. Over the years this company developed into a truly international concern with agents all over the world to handle deliveries of valuable objects as well as households moving abroad. From this developed the travel agency in Moor Lane which still bears the family name. A furniture repository had been built in St. Luke's Road in the 1930s but was destroyed in an air raid in 1941. Its replacement, opened in 1951 was a highly efficient facility to handle carpets and furniture and small valuable items.

The office of the local health board moved to a house at No. 60 Victoria Road in 1863. It later became the office of the Urban District Council for a short time before moving to Alexandra Hall.

A modern sign names the road between Cambridge Road and College Road as Victoria Road West. Cambridge Road was called Sniddle Lane until the 1870s when the first houses were built. A Sniddle is a patch of poor marshland with grass and rushes.

BLUNDELLSANDS

The area known as Blundellsands, originally called Blundell le-sands, was designed by the local architect T. Mellard Reade and surveyor George Goodison. Its transport links and its bracing, healthy air and sea views were to be the attraction for the mansions of the Liverpool nouveau riche. There was to be no industry of any kind, nor shops, only churches. In the centre of the estate was Blundellsands Park, an essential part of the idea of a garden town, as was the insistence by the leaseholders, the Blundell family, that there were to be no paving stones, only grass verges. The first houses were built in 1854 and between then and the 1870s the sweeping crescents and tree lined avenues gradually filled with houses large enough to maintain a full staff and grounds large enough to employ a full time gardener to look after the tennis

courts and croquet lawns as well as the gardens. The leases stated that '...*the residential character of this portion of the township is strictly preserved...although no hard and fast line is drawn, builders must spend between £1,000 and £1,200 on each house built, or £1,800 on a pair. These are, of course minimum not maximum charges and the result is that Blundellsands, from the station to Hall Road, now consists of little else but large and palatial residences for Liverpool's commercial and professional men.*'

The derivations of some of the road names in this area are obvious for instance; Nicholas Road, from the parish church, Burbo Bank from the large sandbank at the mouth of the Mersey. Burbo Crescent was once called Willies Road after William Blundell. Some are not so obvious such as Merrilocks Road from the old English 'myrr' for a swamp and 'loc' for an enclosed piece of land. Before the building of the houses this area had a very large rabbit population. This accounts for names such as Warren Road, Warrenhouse Road and Rabbit Road. This last changed its name to Weld Road in 1927.

The first houses on the estate where built in 1854 close to the railway station. Over the next twenty years many more fine houses were established. Mellard Reade built a house for himself on the corner of Warren Road and the Serpentine, called Park Corner. Treleaven House, built for Nicholas Blundell in 1867, stands on the corner of Warren Road and Blundellsands Road with its distinctive archway. This features the arms of the Blundell family and the initials NB, for Nicholas Blundell and AMB, for his wife Agnes Mary after whom Agnes Road is named. Ramleh in Burbo Bank Road was the home of William Forwood from 1871 to 1898. Of Blundellsands he says; '*Its wide expanse of the sea with its background of the Welsh mountains, Snowdon standing in the far distance, and in the near foreground the constant parade of great merchant ships and steamers which pass and re-pass the day long, make a picture which for beauty and varying interest it is difficult to surpass*'. The Earl of Northbrook, then First Lord of the Admiralty, stayed at Ramleh and said that he knew of no marine view so charming except possibly the Bay of Naples.

The First World War changed the whole fabric of English society. From 1918 the mansions of Blundellsands faced attack from many quarters. Many were affected by the destruction caused by coastal erosion, and many more became the victims of the rising cost of maintenance and the almost total disappearance of domestic staff. Some were turned into private schools, others into flats. By 1930 only a minority were still in use by one family. The trend now is to either demolish and use the site for multiple housing, or convert the house for use as a retirement care home.

The late nineteenth century was noted for the rise in the growth of organised sport throughout the country. In 1860 only cricket and rowing had any kind of structure with nationally agreed rules, by 1885 they were joined by football, rugby, athletics, tennis, golf, cycling, swimming, and even croquet and archery. Organised sport, at this time, was the prerogative of the leisured classes and has its foundation in the public schools and universities. It is no surprise therefore that facilities for sporting activities would feature in the plans for Blundellsands. The All England Croquet Club was formed at Wimbledon in 1869. Lawn tennis was included in its remit but soon took over, the first tennis championships being held there in 1877. Although almost every house had a tennis court and a croquet lawn, a tennis club was an integral part of Blundellsands Park. Other clubs were formed in Dowhills Road and the present site of Waterloo Rugby Club.

The West Lancashire Golf Club was laid out in 1873 and gained a nationwide reputation. It has often been used as a qualifying course for the Open Championship, especially when that international event has been held at Hoylake or Birkdale. The club achieved a world record when the longest hole-in-one was recorded on the 393 yard seventh hole in 1972.

A rugby team from Merchant Taylors School formed a club called the Serpentine, after where they played, in 1882. Apparently the secretary got tired of filling in rabbit holes before every game, as well as being accused of poaching. The club moved to Manley Road in Waterloo in 1884 where they stayed until1906 apart from temporary residence at the Old Crosby Cricket Club ground from

1893 to 1898. In 1906 the club, by now called Waterloo Rugby Club moved to the ex-Northern Cricket Club premises in Haig Road. The club was established at its current home in March 1921.

Blundellsands Sailing Club was founded in 1899 as the Altmouth Sailing Club. It closed in 1901 and was revived in 1907 as the Burbo Sailing Club. Because sailing was forbidden during the First World War, he |club closed in 1914 and re-opened as the Blundellsands Sailing Club in 1921. It is still going strong today.

The only commercial enterprise allowed in Blundellsands was the Hotel. With the massive growth of the railways it was common practice to provide a hotel conveniently placed near a station. This hotel was opened in 1870. 1881 saw the move of Blundellsands station to opposite the hotel, as well as a considerable surge in the house building in the area. For most of its life the Blundellsands Hotel was recognised as one of the best hotels on Merseyside and the 'B.S.' was a regular meeting place for the people of Crosby. The impressive function facility, the Mauritania Room, and the large ballroom were great assets to the area and provided many jobs. However it finally closed its doors in March 2001 and is now redeveloped as retirement flats. The original façade has been retained but that is little compensation for the loss of a well known feature of the town. Also adjacent to the station is one of Crosby's military links. The Royal Artillery 'Gunners

Club' in Byron Road was opened just after the Second World War

Blundellsands now boasts a state of the art leisure centre right on the beach, which replaced the crumbling swimming baths which had been opened in the early 1960s

BRIGHTON-LE-SANDS

With the growth in the acknowledgement of the recreational and health advantages of sea bathing, the area to the north of Liverpool was striving to match the delights of the south coast of England. In the early 1800s, Brighton-le-sands was just a handful of isolated fisherman's cottages. When it was given the name Little Brighton in about 1840 it had a population of less than 150. More cottages were built with the road names reflecting the competition with the south coast. Brighton Vale, Sussex Street and Worthing Street were being built, as was a road to run parallel to the shore. What is now Oxford Road was called Brighton Road and Mersey View and Bridge Road, Little Brighton. Warrenhouse Road, which ran down to the sea from Little Brighton, had at least one shop and a pub – the Ship Inn. By 1845 the population was approaching 200 and it had a second pub – the original Royal Oak. (the present Royal Oak was built on the same site in the 1920s). The Ship Inn was often used for meetings of the town's officers. It was closed in about 1925 and was derelict for some years. It was finally demolished in 1961. The site is now occupied by the flats Warrenhouse Court. More shops, some selling fresh sea food, and a village school had arrived by 1860. 1874 saw the building of St. Nicholas Church, and within five years Harlech Road, Cavendish Road and many of the three storey shops on Bridge Road were in place. With this came the change of name to Brighton-le-sands. It is now a thriving but independent community. Although the last remaining motor car dealers – Hepburn's has gone to be replaced by yet more flats, and the post office went in January 2005, there is a move to reinstate the name with official boundaries.

This is not an area that you would normally associate with the 'Sport of Kings'. The first record of horse racing in Crosby was in 1577. This was probably only a two horse race but was to be an annual event held every Ascension Day. In the event it appears that only this first one took place. The course was a four and a half mile straight line along the Crosby Marsh and the sand dunes between Crosby and Bank Hall. It followed the approximate line of Bridge Road, Mersey View and Oxford Road. There may have been a few races until the next record of 1654. In that year William Blundell measured, or 'stooped out', an oval shaped course which included the start of the 1577 course. A map of 1786 shows the Race Course as roughly the circuit now occupied by Alexandra Park, Mersey Road, Oxford Road, Brooke Road and back along College Road. 1654 was the height of the English Civil War and Cromwell's Commonwealth had forbade all sports, including horse racing. Blundell had the full support of the Molyneux family, who were not only

recusants but Royalists to a man. As owners of a huge swathe of Lancashire between them they obviously felt fairly secure. William was imprisoned and exiled but returned to Crosby with the Restoration of Charles II in 1660. It is possible that odd races were held on the course until 1682 when official rules and regulations were drawn up. One of these, a common rule throughout the country was that a horse could not be considered a winner until it had passed the winning post before the second horse reached the 'distance post', some 240 yards back. This is the origin of the phrase 'to win by a distance'. The racing went on intermittently until about 1786. The 1786 map clearly shows the grandstand at about where St. Nicholas. Church now stands. There have been comments that the house called Standfield in Liverpool Road was so named because it was on the site of this stand. If the map is correct this supposition is impossible. During the 1760s and 1770s race days had a carnival atmosphere, with many fast food booths and a flourishing gambling scene. Crowds arrived by boat from Liverpool by sea, and by the new canal. More crowds walked or rode up from the city along the seashore. Unfortunately this all attracted a large criminal element and the Crosby races went the way of the other Crosby carnival, the Goose Feast. The 1816 enclosure of Crosby Marsh and Blundellsands effectively killed off what was left of this colourful part of Crosby's history. Horse racing carried on along the sands until about 1838 but this was a very low key amateurish effort

CHAPTER 7
CROSBY SEASHORE

Although Great Crosby was initially an inland village, separated from the Mersey estuary and the Irish Sea by inhospitable marshland, the sea has always played a part in its history. As in most of this part of Lancashire the coastline was apt to change quite dramatically and with very little warning. The prevailing north-west winds were capable of producing tremendous tidal surges, the small village of Argameols, on the sea side of Formby, was washed away, almost overnight in the early 1500s. As Liverpool's importance increased so did the volume of shipping using the Mersey estuary. The ever changing configuration of channels and sand bars caused by repeated alteration of the course of the River Alt caused many accidents resulting in loss of life and property. Something had to be done – the newly rich ship owners were beginning to lose money. The first step was to dredge a wide, clearly marked channel on the Crosby side of the Mersey estuary. This was named the Victoria Channel in honour of the new queen. One of Britain's earliest lighthouses was built on the sand between Hightown and Formby. This was replaced in October 1839 by a wooden structure in the Hightown dunes just north of Crosby. Another of the ubiquitous prefabricated iron structures so beloved of this Victorian period was planned but came to nought. In November 1846 it was finally replaced by a brick built tower seventy four

feet high. This had an oil burning lamp and five mirror lamps. On the night of one fierce gale in February 1898 the wind blew in the windows of the lantern room. The mirror lamps exploded and the mass of burning oil set fire to the lantern room floor, and then through the building. Within fifteen minutes the whole tower was ablaze and there was no escape for the keeper on duty, Robert Buckley, his wife, Mary Ann, a friend Mrs. Alice Clements of Hoylake, and the Buckley's collie dog. Although a temporary light was set up, it only lasted six months and then Crosby lighthouse was no more.

The first life boat station in the country was opened at Formby in 1776. It closed in 1915 and, after serving some time as a café, was finally demolished in 1965.

A coast guard station was established at the end of Mariners Road on the site of the present leisure centre, in 1861. This was closed down in 1924 and sold by auction, although apparently only the coast guard officer's house was habitable. One of the coast guards defected to become the first caretaker of the West Lancs Golf Club when it opened in 1873. A brand new station was opened in 1982 to cover all shipping between North Wales and Morecambe Bay. In 1890 the Admiralty set up four measured mile land-marks off the coast. The original purpose was to check the speed specifications of newly

LEFT Beachside Towers, Blundellsands, 1921.

built naval vessels coming from the Merseyside ship-yards. Only those at the bottom of Mariners Road and Hall Road still survive. Naturally any other ship owner who wished to check the speed of his ships could use them. A small rent was paid by the Admiralty to the Blundell estate who owned the foreshore.

The LV (Light Vessel), 'Comet' was built at the John Brown shipyard on the Clyde in 1904 to serve as a lightship in the Bay of Dublin. It eventually ended up in Liverpool Bay as the Crosby Lightship. In 1965 it was sold to a group of entrepreneurs who converted it into a pirate radio vessel, 'Radio Scotland'. As with most of the other pirate stations it was closed down by act of Parliament in 1967. It was broken up at the Van der Marel yard in Holland in 1969.

Another problem brought by the north-west winds was that of drifting sand. The few farmers who were trying to scratch a living from the marsh lands were now faced with having their land covered with ever increasing sand dunes. This got worse with the excessive number of storms affecting the area in the early seventeen hundreds. An answer was needed and where else to look than Holland. The Dutch had been fighting a battle with the sea for centuries. By the thirteenth century they had gained much experience in the use of marram grass for dune stabilization, and were happy to share this. From about 1570 the planting of marram, or starr grass became a feature of the Crosby coast, as it still is; but there was a big problem. This grass was very useful for making mats, baskets, and other domestic use, even repairing thatched roofs. As fast as it was planted in the dunes it was 'harvested' by the locals. In 1637 this became a criminal offence. Officials were appointed called 'haweslookers' who wandered the dunes looking for people illegally cutting grass. By 1710 it became a requirement for land owners to plant marram – from 1730 they could be fined for not doing so. An Act of Parliament of 1742 made cutting of grass, and negligence in its maintenance a criminal offence. This was a little late for the ancient village of Ravenmeols which was buried under tons of sand during a storm of 1739.

Over the nineteenth century the vagaries of climate, the development of the Crosby shoreline, even the increasing number of trippers coming up from Liverpool by the new railway to sample the sea air were all blamed for the frequent changes in the course of the River Alt. The river's estuary moved from as far south of the Gladstone Dock area to Formby. When the railway opened, in 1848, there were no houses along the sea front between 'Sandheys', where the avenue of that name now runs, and the Crosby lighthouse. This was soon to change. The Blundellsands area with its fine wide roads and large detached houses was being developed from the 1860s. One of its main features was the road called the Serpentine. Constructed in 1888 this linked the two stations, Hall Road and Crosby, and, in between, swept round towards

the sea. This gave the opportunity to build some of the area's finest houses with an uninterrupted sea view of the Welsh hills and the fascinating panorama of Liverpool's shipping. There was however a price to be paid, not just the recommended £1200 for each house. By 1907 the erosion of land caused by the changing flow of the Alt, which was now running parallel to the shoreline, was causing some concern. In that year the sea had encroached three and a half feet as measured at the Hall Road landmark. This encroachment averaged 33 feet per year between 1913 and 1920, and 38 feet per year between 1920 and 1928. South Esk was built in 1907 and by 1920 had lost its tennis court and croquet lawn, and the house itself was only sixteen feet from the sea. By 1925 South Esk, Beachside Towers, Netherwood, Red House, Holmside and Edgewater had all been vacated and demolished, their foundations swept into the sea. Burbo Bank Road itself lost half its carriageway in the Spring tides of 1931. In the 1920s it was became a popular if some-

RIGHT Beachside Towers about to fall into the sea, 1923.

what macabre entertainment to catch a bus or train from Liverpool to watch the fine houses of the super rich falling into the waves. A sort of local 'schadenfreude'! Some of these houses survived the coastal erosion to eventually fall victim to the economic tide which made such large houses, and the necessary staff to run them, no longer viable. Holyrood House was demolished in 1969 to make way for a block of modern flats, although the name was retained.

The Crosby Council tried to remodel itself on King Canute but had no more success. Large amounts of tin slag from a factory in Bootle were used to form a wall to train the Alt away towards Hightown. This was moderately successful but it was not until 1936 that a proper training wall was built – or maybe the river decided on a change of direction itself? An extra help to build up the sea defences came from 1942 onwards as rubble from bombed properties was dumped there. Most of the bricks and slates now found along the sea shore are from this source. The building of a new sea wall in the 1970s largely solved the problem

Fort Crosby was built on the sandhills between Hall Road and Hightown in 1906. Its purpose, along with its opposite construction, Fort Perch Rock, New Brighton, was to defend the approaches to the port of Liverpool. It saw no action in the First World War and was used after 1918 as a gunnery training centre. The unit of the Lancashire and Cheshire Heavy Brigade of the Royal Artillery based there were also responsible for the defence of Barrow-in-Furness. By 1940 the heavy guns were supplemented by an array of searchlights and anti-aircraft guns. The Fort saw little action and after the war was adapted to house German prisoners of war. The prisoners left in 1950 and the Territorial Army used the Fort for training until 1954. It was closed in 1957 and eventually demolished ten years later.

Crosby was never in any sense a port, provided you do not count the flagging down of passing ships for a lift to Ireland. The area was considered an ideal place for marine personalities to live because of its nearness to Liverpool, bracing sea air, and of course the sight of ships passing to and from the port.

William Thomas Turner was born in Liverpool in 1856. He was captain of the 'Lusitania' when it was sunk by a German U-boat off Ireland on 7th May 1915. Over 1200 lives were lost. Turner was last to leave the stricken ship and died at his home, 50 De Villiers Avenue, in 1933. His son Peter was lost when his ship was torpedoed in World War II within a mile of the spot where the 'Lusitania' sank.

Charles Alfred Bartlett was born in London in 1868. His career at sea brought him to Merseyside in 1900 and he and his family moved to 7 Thorpes Lane (now Coronation Road). They had various addresses, 5 Winstanley Road, Waterloo, 13 Regent Road, Crosby, 'Montclair', Rabbit Road, Crosby (now Weld Road) ending up at 15 Victoria

Road, Waterloo. He supervised the arrangements for the maiden voyage of the 'Titanic' and was to have been her captain after this voyage, Captain Edward John Smith's last command. Captain Smith was living at 17 Marine Terrace, Waterloo when he set sail on the 'Titanic'. He went down with the ship. The White Star Line launched a replacement for the 'Titanic', the 'Britannic', in 1914. This was even bigger and incorporated all the lessons learnt from the 1912 tragedy. Bartlett was made captain and the ship was immediately commandeered by the government as a hospital ship. She made five voyages bringing home wounded from the Gallipoli campaign. On 21st November 1916, during the sixth voyage, an explosion of unknown cause sank the ship, which went down within minutes. Fortunately it was on an outward journey to collect wounded so only thirty people lost their lives. Bartlett was the last to leave the ship and retired to 22 Marine Crescent, Waterloo. He moved to 'Lynwood', Serpentine, and finally 31 Warwick Avenue. He died in Park House Nursing Home in 1945.

Joseph Bruce Ismay was born at Enfield House, Endbutt Lane in 1862, but was brought up at 13 Beach Lawn, Waterloo. He succeeded his father as Chief Executive of the White Star Line in 1899 and travelled as a passenger on the 'Titanic'. As the ship sank he helped many into lifeboats and only escaped when he was as sure as possible that there were no women and children left. After receiving some criticism for cowardice, he retired to London and died a broken man in 1937.

Other members of the crew of the 'Titanic' had Crosby connections. Chief Engineer Joseph Bell lived at 1 Belvidere Road. He and his engineers manned the pumps and kept the ship afloat for an extra one and a half hours, thereby saving many lives and sacrificing their own. There is a plaque to his memory in St. Faith's church. Second Officer Charles Herbert Lightoller of 8 Cambridge Avenue, Second Engineer Bertie Wilson, old boy of Merchant Taylor's School of 16 Norma Road, Chief Steward Andrew Latimer of 4 Glenwyllin Road and Assistant Purser John Rice of 37 Kimberley Drive, all lost their lives on that night.

In 1910 Henry George Kendall was captain of the steamship 'Montrose' sailing from Liverpool to Quebec. Among his passengers were a rather odd couple. They had boarded as a father and son but did not act like it. Kendall became convinced they were in fact the wanted wife murderer Crippen and his lover/secretary Ethel le Neve. The 'Montrose' was one of the first ships to be fitted with wireless telegraphy. Using this he informed Scotland Yard of his suspicions. Inspector Dew, who was in charge of the case, boarded the liner 'Laurentic', at Liverpool and pursued the 'Montrose' across the Atlantic. He caught up with and boarded the 'Montrose' as she entered the St. Lawrence River, recognised Crippen and arrested him. Crippen was hanged for the murder on 23rd

November 1910 but as he left Kendall's ship he shouted a curse at the captain. By May 1914 Kendall was captain of the 'Empress of Ireland', and lived at 3 Harlech Road, Crosby. As the ship passed out of the St. Lawrence on its way from Quebec to Liverpool, passing the spot where Crippen was arrested, a sudden fog came down and the 'Empress' collided with a Norwegian cargo vessel. Kendall's ship sank within fifteen minutes, he survived but nearly 900 people, including 134 children, did not. This still stands as the worst ever peacetime shipping disaster in terms of passengers lost. He retired and went to live at 40 Brooke Road, Waterloo and died in a London nursing home in 1965

One cannot leave the Crosby sea shore without mention of one of the areas' most notable eccentrics. Jack Johnson moved to Crosby about 1865 and built himself a house of driftwood on the beach. This later sported a brick fireplace and chimney. His address was Alt Cottage, Hall Road – I doubt whether he ever had, or even sought, planning permission. He subsisted on selling driftwood and cockles, presumably tolerated by the fearsome cockle mollies. His nickname was Roast Beef from the colour of his permanently wind- and sun-tanned face. He died about 1918; Alt Cottage was an early victim of the shifting sands.

We have looked at Crosby all the way from the Boundary Cottage in Little Crosby Road to the Boundary Club, re-opened as La Barbacoa in 1982, at Brighton-le-sands. I hope that you enjoyed the journey.

BIBLIOGRAPHY

Ashton, William. *Battle of land and sea.* 1909

Ashton, William. *Evolution of a coastline.* 1920

Barge, J. *A Gazetteer of Liverpool breweries.* 1987

Barnes, Thomas. *Changes from 1860 to 1910 along the banks of the River Mersey.* Edited by Allan Johnston c.1991

Barrow, J.P. *Crosby Lighthouse.* 1955

Blundell, Margaret. *A Lancashire Squire.* Edited by Mark Blundell. 2002

Blundell, Nicholas. *The Great Diurnal of Nicholas Blundell.* (3 vols) Edited by F.Tyrer 1968

Blundell, William. *Cavalier; letters of William Blundell 1620–1698.* 1933

Bulman, Joe. *My Hightown 1897–1969.* 3rd edition revised 2003

Edwards, B.J.N. *The Vikings in North West England* 1998

Farthing, Andrew. *Essential history of Crosby and Thornton.* 1997

Forbes, N.N. *A Century of transport in Crosby and district.* c.1956 typewritten

Forwood, Sir W.B. *Some recollections of a busy life.* 1910

Gresswell, R. Kay. *Sandy shores in South Lancashire.* 1953

Harding, Stephen. *Viking Mersey.* 2002

Heath, Tom. *Crosby, Seaforth and Waterloo Parts 1 and 2.* 2000-2001

Hollinghurst, H. *Chesterfield High School; the first twenty five years 1972–1997.* 1998

Hull, Roger. *Social differentiation in a North Liverpool suburb; the case of Great Crosby and Waterloo.*

Jesson, Walter. *Betwixt Ribbel and Moerse.* 1982

Lamb, Charles. *History of Crosby.* 1936

Lewis, J.R. *The Birth of Waterloo.* Revised edition 1982

Luft, H. M. *A History of Merchant Taylors' School, Crosby 1620–1970.* 1970

Merchant Taylors Girls School. *John Harrison and his school.* 1929

Miller, John S.C. *The story of the church in Great Crosby.* 1937

Murray, Brenda. *From Liverpool Merchant to Country Squire; notes on the Myers family.* 2003

Pinfold, John. *Gallant sport; the authentic history of Liverpool Races and the Grand National.* 1999

Reade, T. Mellard. *1st report of the Royal Commission on coast erosion.* 1907

Reade, T. Mellard. *The gypsum boulder of Great Crosby.* 1898

Roberts, Stan. *The Liverpool telephone area story.* 1981

St. Luke's History Group. *St. Luke's Church, Great Crosby 1853–2003.* 2003

Smith, Philip. *The sands of time.* 1999

Stanistreet, Jennifer and Farthing, Andrew. *Crosby in camera.* 1993

Taylor, Henry. *Ancient wells and crosses.* 1906

Tyrer, Frank. *Windmills of Crosby.* 1972

Tyrer, Frank. *Let's walk to Little Crosby.* Revised edition, Sefton 1992

Tyrer, Frank and Miller, J.Allen. *Notes on the history of Crosby.* c.1965

Williams, Thomas. *Some events and personalities concerned with the parish of Sefton and the Free Grammar School (Merchant Taylor's) at Great Crosby 1755–1811.* Historic Society of Lancashire and Cheshire Vol. 104

Wotherspoon, David. *Mighty Mariners; the story of Marine A.F.C.* 1997

LEFT The present site of the village cross.

LIST OF ILLUSTRATIONS

For a complete list of picture acknowledgements, please see page 6.

INDEX